THE TENNIS
DOCTOR

THE TENNIS DOCTOR

Alexander McNab

Illustrations by Michael Brent

A JOHN BOSWELL
ASSOCIATES BOOK

Villard Books New York 1993

Published in the United States by Villard Books,
a division of Random House, Inc., New York, and
simultaneously in Canada by Random House of
Canada Limited, Toronto. Villard Books is a regis-
tered trademark of Random House, Inc.

*Designed by Nan Jernigan/ The Colman Press
Cover Design by Richard Rossiter
Cover case manufactured by S.D. Leather
Goods Inc,. Hackensack, N.J.*

ISBN 0-679-41993-4

Library of Congress Cataloging-In-Publication Data

McNab, Alexander
   The tennis doctor / Alexander McNab.
      p. cm.
   ISBN 0-679-41993-4
   1. Tennis.   I. Title.
GV99.M373   1993
796.342-dc20   92-56835

Manufactured in the United States of America

9 8 7 6 5 4 3 2

First Edition

To the memory of my parents,
Mary and Jim McNab,
who supported and encouraged
my interests in tennis
and journalism.

ACKNOWLEDGMENTS

This book could not have been completed without the wisdom and counsel of the following people:

My mentors: Arthur Ashe, Peter Burwash, Billie Jean King, Stan Smith, Tony Trabert, and Dennis Van der Meer, great champions and master teaching professionals with whom I've been privileged to collaborate on instruction writing for more than a decade.

Julie Anthony, Roy Barth, Vic Braden, Tim Gullikson, Jack Groppel, and Jim Loehr, experts whose instruction writing I've edited and sources who have never been too busy to share their knowledge of the game in interviews I've requested over the years.

Tracy Leonard, who taught me most of what I know about racquets, strings, and things, and Tom Brunick, the self-described "shoe geek."

Donna Doherty, Editor of *Tennis* magazine, dear friend and indefatigable mixed doubles partner.

Susan Adams, who guided me gracefully through more than three years of "On Your Own" tennis columns for the Sports Monday section of the *New York Times*.

Steve Goethner, the Macintosh maven who solved my computer problems.

Barry Tarshis, who recommended me for this project.

Bob Bruns, Richard Buonomo, Hector Garrido, Shelly Holson, Mindy Jeruss, Jim and Norma Kane, Jerry McLaughlin, Perry Seamonds, Larry Staiger, and Mike Vartuli, proofreaders, critics, computer helpers, doubles partners, and all good friends on and off the court.

CONTENTS

Chapter 2: Backhand   45

BACKHAND   45

The Step-by-Step Basics   45

Chapter 3: Serve

Chapter 5: Competing 118

INTRODUCTION

This book is written to help tennis players of all abilities hit all of the essential shots, correct common stroking errors, and incorporate the nuances of pace, spin, trajectory, and court position into their shot-making. It also includes a brief primer on some elements of match play and a few ideas about practice, conditioning, and equipment.

The book is organized as an easy-access guide to the fundamentals of sound stroking and the cures for common tennis ills. The first four Chapters cover the strokes: FOREHAND, BACKHAND, SERVE (and return of serve), and NET PLAY (volley, overhead, lob, and touch shots). Each stroke section begins with a review of the basics of the shot in step-by-step progression. Next are quick-fix ideas to improve your overall consistency with the stroke. Then come simple tips to eliminate the everyday errors of hitting into the net, hitting long, and hitting wide. Last is a list of other frequent problems on a particular stroke and their cures.

The winner of a tennis match at all but the elite level is the player who makes the fewer errors. The best way to correct a faulty stroke and reduce your errors is to focus on *one fundamental idea* during the swing. That one idea can just as easily be one of the basic components of the stroke as a suggested correction. So reviewing the basic instructions at the start of each section can be as helpful as consulting the quick fixes, simple tips, and cures for frequent problems that follow. In fact, you may find the immediate answer you need just by scanning the headings in the Contents.

The fifth Chapter deals with aspects of COMPETING (strategy, mental pointers, playing left-handers, court surfaces, doubles, rules questions, and tiebreakers), plus information on practice, conditioning and equipment.

The goal of this book is to lead you to more consistent shot-making, better results, and greater enjoyment when you step on the court.

A NOTE TO LEFT-HANDERS

Please note that this book is written and illustrated from a right-handed player's perspective. A lefty should reverse all right and left directional instructions in the stroking sections, as well as all clock-face designations (i.e., 2 o'clock becomes 10 o'clock). The lefty can exact revenge for this inconvenience with a sinister wide slice serve to a righty's backhand.

FOREHAND

BASIC SET-UP TERMS

1. Stances

The preferred, classic way to hit the ball on most ground strokes is with a *closed stance.* Turn and make your final step to the ball across and forward with the left foot on a forehand and with the right foot on a backhand. Your feet are roughly aligned perpendicular to the net and your weight is on your front foot at impact.

Closed stance

The other way, used by many modern players especially on the forehand, is an *open stance*. Your final step to the ball is with the right foot on a forehand and the left foot on a backhand. Your feet are aligned more parallel with the net and your weight is on your back foot at impact.

Open stance

2. Swing Paths

Although it may not look like it, on almost every ground stroke you hit from your baseline the ball must go *up* to clear the net. You control the trajectory of your shot and determine the type of spin it has by the swing path you use.

A *flat swing path* has a slight upward trajectory from the end of your backswing through impact and into the follow-through.

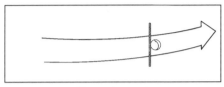

Flat swing path

A *low-to-high swing path* has a more exaggerated upward arc from the end of your backswing through impact and into the follow-through. It is the swing path for topspin.

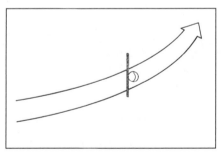

Low-to-high swing path

A *high-to-low swing path* has a descending arc from the end of the back-swing through impact into the beginning of the follow-through, but it rises again gradually near the end of the follow-through, like a shallow check mark. It is the swing path for a slice.

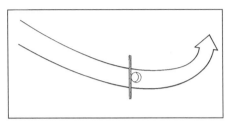

High-to-low swing path

3. Racquet-Face Alignments

The angle or alignment of the racquet face at impact also affects your shot. An *open* racquet-face alignment means the strings are tilted up slightly toward the sky as the strings meet the ball. A *square* racquet-face alignment means the strings are perpendicular to the court as they meet the ball. A *closed* racquet-face alignment means the strings are tilted slightly down

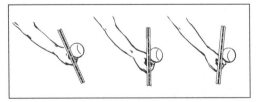

| *Open* racquet-face alignment | *Square* racquet-face alignment | *Closed* racquet-face alignment |

as they meet the ball. Another way of describing a closed face is a hooded face.

FOREHAND

The Step-by-Step Basics

1. Grips

The most popular forehand grip is the *Eastern*. It is also called the shake-hands grip because you get it by holding the racquet with your other hand so the strings are perpendicular to the court and then shaking hands with the handle with your hitting hand. It puts the palm of your hand right behind the handle at impact. Another way to get this grip is to hold the racquet as before with your other hand, lay your hitting palm flat against the strings, and then slide your hand straight down the shaft and grip the handle. The Eastern is a stable, versatile grip for shots of all heights and spins because it keeps the racquet face in square alignment throughout the swing.

The *semi-Western* and *Western* grips are used by many young pros with powerful forehands. The hand is turned much farther under the handle on the Western (a little less so on the semi-Western) than on the Eastern. It is sometimes called a "frying-pan" grip, because you get it by laying your racquet flat on a tabletop and then picking it up as if lifting a frying pan.

The semi-Western and Western grips put the racquet face in more of a closed alignment. They are best for medum-to high-bouncing shots and for generating topspin. They can be the most user-friendly grips for powerful forehands, but require the biggest shift to a proper backhand grip.

The *Continental* grip puts more of the palm on top of the handle as you hold the racquet on edge. It is halfway between an Eastern forehand and an Eastern backhand. Many players who use the Continental use it for all shots. Because it aligns the racquet face in a slightly open position during the forehand swing, the Continental requires expert timing and sometimes even some extra wrist movement to hit the ball squarely. It is best on low-bouncing balls and crosscourt shots, but it makes hitting high shots and some down-the-line shots quite difficult.

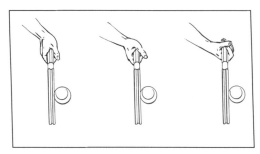

Continental   *Eastern*   *Semi-Western*
forehand grip   *forehand grip*   *forehand grip*

2. The Basic Image

Think of your racquet as a natural extension of your arm. The basic motion of the forehand, then, is swinging your arm back and then forward to strike the ball and drive it across the net with your open palm. The Eastern grip most easily allows you to do that with the racquet.

3. The Ready Position

The ready position at the baseline should enable you to turn quickly to prepare for either a forehand or a backhand. Stand with your weight on the balls of your feet, which should be about shoulder width apart. Your knees should be flexed. Don't bend over too far from the waist. That will hurt your balance and slow you down when moving for a wide shot.

Baseline Ready Position: Your weight should be on the balls of your feet.

Hold your racquet *loosely* with either an Eastern or Continental grip so you can turn with equal speed for a forehand or backhand. Cradle the racquet with your left hand at the intersection of the shaft and racquet head, with the racquet almost parallel to the court. You might even extend the index finger of your other hand up onto the strings. It will help you keep the racquet head from drooping, assist you as you shift grips, and guide the racquet head back in the early part of the backswing.

4. The Initial Turn & Pivot

As soon as you see the ball leave your opponent's strings and sense that it is coming to your forehand side, begin turning your shoulders and pivot on your right foot. Coil until your shoulders and hips are perpendicular to the net. Your front shoulder (the left) should point at your opponent as you complete your backswing. Your weight should shift fully onto your right leg. You should complete the turn by the time the ball bounces on your side of the court.

5. Lay Your Wrist Back

As you turn, set the racquet by laying your wrist back. That puts the racquet head behind your hand as you take the racquet back and swing forward. You want to maintain that angle into impact. But you don't want to cock the racquet so far back that the only way to square up at impact is to snap your wrist forward.

Wrist-Raquet Angle: Keep your wrist laid back into contact.

6. Straight Back or Loop?

Some players take the racquet straight back and swing straight forward, as if opening and closing a gate. This no-frills approach to the backswing has few things that can go wrong, is especially good for flat or underspin forehands, and is ideal for handling fast shots.

Other players prefer to take the racquet back in a loop or circling path, with the racquet head high early in the preparation phase, then low at the end of the back-swing and rising again on the forward swing. They find the loop backswing gives their stroke a smoother rhythm and a greater potential for power and topspin.

The loop requires better timing than the straight backswing, which makes it easier to use on slow shots than fast ones, when you may not have enough time for such elaborate preparation.

In either case, unless you are hitting a slice or underspin forehand, your racquet should follow a rising trajectory on the forward swing so the ball will clear the net.

7. Line Up the Ball with the Racquet Butt

Regardless of what grip or type of backswing you use, at the end of your forehand backswing your elbow should be bent and tucked in pretty close to your body and the butt of your racquet handle should point at the ball. That indicates your wrist and hand are in the right place and you haven't taken the racquet too far back around your body.

End of backswing: Line up the ball with the racquet butt.

8. Step, Then Swing

Your first move forward should be with your feet. Step in and across with your left leg and drive into the shot with your knees. Let your forward step trigger your forward swing, not the reverse. Also, think of an anchor grounding your back (right) foot to the court. Don't raise the anchor until you are well into the follow-through.

9. Maintain the Wrist-Racquet Angle

On the forward swing, your racquet head should trail your body and arm into impact. The preset angle between your racquet and wrist should result in a square alignment at impact. Try to maintain the angle as long you can through the contact zone. Your racquet head should move ahead of your wrist only in the later stages of the follow-through. Avoid snapping the racquet head through with just your wrist.

10. Point of Contact

On the forehand, your point of contact with the ball should be anywhere from even with your navel to even with the toes of your left foot. It also should be close enough to your body so your elbow is comfortably bent for additional leverage. Two common mistakes to avoid are contacting the ball too far back in your stance and contacting the ball too far away, which would make your arm straight at impact.

Point of Contact: Meet the ball between your navel and the toes of your left foot.

11. Drive Your Palm Toward the Target

Recalling the image of your open palm hitting the ball over the net, think of driving your palm forward toward the target as you hit and follow through. The idea is to keep your strings facing the target for as long as possible, which enhances both power and control. To get that feeling of extending ahead, think of hitting through six balls in a line toward your target.

12. Keep Your Head Down

A routine error most players make is not watching the ball closely. Contact happens in a matter of milliseconds and the ball and racquet are moving too fast for you to actually see them meet. But you still should keep your eyes focused on the point where you think contact will occur. On the forehand, the tendency is to look up too soon to see where your shot is going. That causes you to pull your head up, which may move your racquet off-line. The result is either an error, a mis-hit, or a weak shot. To avoid this mistake, keep your head down and your eyes focused on the point of contact until well into your follow through.

13. Finish High

The photographs you see of pros with their racquet faces closed and their racquet arms wrapped over their left shoulders at the end of their forehands are deceiving. All that occurs well after the ball has left the strings and the arm and racquet head have stopped accelerating toward the target. You should think of finishing high on the forehand to ensure you drive the ball up and over the net. Imagine your chin resting on your bicep as you complete the stroke.

The Quick Fix

1. Relax Your Arm and Swing, Don't Slap

The most common cause of an erratic forehand is too much reliance on just your arm and/or wrist and not enough use of your body in preparing for the shot and swinging forward. You may be either stiff-arming the ball or snapping your racquet head through with just a flick of the wrist. So keep your arm relaxed and think swing, not slap.

Correcting the Everyday Errors

1. Hitting into the Net

Aim higher. Bend your knees. Open the racquet face. Swing out toward the target. Make a higher follow-through.

2. Hitting Long

Keep your head still. Close the racquet face a little. Add some topspin (see page 39 for tips).

3. Hitting Wide Crosscourt

Make a fuller turn. Keep your wrist laid back at impact. Swing forward toward the target, not across your body.

4. Hitting Wide Down the Line

Turn sooner and get the racquet back earlier. Shift your weight forward. Make contact farther in front. Make a full forward follow-through.

Five Frequent Problems and Their Cures

1. Insufficient Topspin

Swing on a steeper low-to-high path. That makes the strings brush up the back of the ball at impact, imparting forward rotation to the ball. To do it:

1) *Try a semi-Western or Western grip.* It will keep the racquet face closed through your preparation and deliver it to the ball in a square alignment at impact. An Eastern grip coming from well below the ball might result in an open racquet face on impact.

2) *Try an open stance.* It will put you in a comfortable position with your Western grip when you make contact with the ball.

3) *Take the racquet back with your elbow up, your palm down, and the racquet face closed.* Imagine the strings facing the ground on the backswing. They will naturally square up as the racquet moves upward and forward through impact.

4) *Make a bigger loop on your back-swing.* Think of your racquet making a big circle. It will increase the racquet-head speed.

Topspin Forehand: Use a loop backswing with a closed racquet face.

5) *Drop the racquet head down at the end of the backswing.* Imagine a line extending on a rising angle straight out of the butt cap of your racquet, through the oncoming ball, and over the net. The steeper the swing path, the more spin you'll get.

6) *Really rotate your hips and shoulders into the shot.* The faster your big muscles move, the faster your wrist and

racquet will move. The end result is more spin and more speed on your shot.

7) *Don't roll the wrist over.* You cannot create consistent topspin by snapping your wrist across or consciously turning the racquet over at impact. Let the racquet face close naturally on your follow-through.

8) *Finish up and out.* You want spin, but you also want depth. So as the racquet keeps climbing on its upward path, it also should keep traveling forward toward your target. If your forehand starts to land short because of too much spin, flatten the arc of the swing a little.

2. Ineffective Approach Shots

Use a slice forehand for control and to make the ball bounce low, which will make it harder for your opponent to hit a passing shot. Swing on a high-to-low path, beginning with a slightly open racquet face, and accelerate the racquet out toward the target. Remain sideways and keep moving forward throughout the stroke. Think of pushing the racquet forward to the spot you want the ball to land. If you cut across your body, you lose depth, pace, and accuracy.

3. When Opponent's Shots Pin You Deep

Hit on the rise. By meeting the ball before it reaches the top of its bounce, you can play closer to the baseline and turn your opponent's power around on him. To do it:

1) *Take a shorter, straighter backswing.* You don't have time for a long loop.

2) *Use a firm grip or the speed of the incoming shot may push your racquet off-line.*

3) *Meet the ball with your racquet and weight forward.* The shorter swing means less racquet-head speed. Your forward momentum will compensate for that lost power source.

4) *Hood the racquet face or the ball will shoot off the strings out of control.*

5) *Play to a "1-2" cadence.* The timing of the shot is a quick "bounce-hit." A regular forehand is closer to a leisurely "bounce and hit."

6) *Remember to follow through.* You must keep swinging the racquet forward for depth and control.

4. High Balls

Prepare high and finish high. The tendency is to try to hit down on the ball. Instead, swing on a straight line, as if you were sweeping books off a high shelf with your racquet. And forget about topspin. There's no way to finish your swing higher than where it started when the ball has bounced to eye level.

5. Hitting on the Run

Accelerate to the ball. Your first step is key. When the ball is wide, you cannot side-shuffle to it. Instead, pivot on your right leg, then accelerate with a long crossover stride with the left leg. That gets your weight, center of gravity, and momentum headed in the right direction. From there:

1) *Run fairly erect, then get low.* It's a more efficient way of moving than hunching over like a chicken pecking along the ground. That will tax your leg muscles heavily.You want to stay in balance by keeping your body over your feet as you move and as you bend your knees to hit.

2) *Pump your arms.* That's what a sprinter does. You may make a later backswing than you would on a normal forehand, but it should promote a contin- uous stroke. You cannot run as fast with your racquet all the way back.

Hitting on the Run: Pump your arms like a sprinter.

3) *Move in diagonally.* You will cut off the angle of your opponent's shot and get some forward momentum into your return. You sacrifice court position and pace by running sideways straight along the baseline.

4) *Let your racquet arm swing freely.* You cannot make a full-body pivot hitting on the run, so your arm has to do the work. Keep it relaxed to make a long, flowing swing with a full follow-through.

5) *Allow for drift.* When you are pulled wide on the dead run, your easiest shot is down the line. Your sideways momentum will carry your shot wide unless you aim a little farther than normal toward the center of the court .

BACKHAND

BACKHAND

The Step-by-Step Basics

1. Grips

The most stable one-handed backhand grip is the *Eastern* backhand. To reach it, turn your hand to the left from an Eastern forehand grip past the Continental grip position until the "V" between your thumb and index finger rests on the top left bevel of the handle. Some players then extend their thumbs farther up the handle than others; it is a matter of personal preference. You do get additional stability by spreading your fingers a little rather than bunching them up. All one-handed backhand grips are inherently weaker than forehand grips

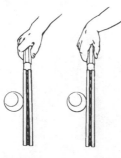

Eastern backhand grip   *Continental backhand grip*

45

because the palm is not behind the handle. However, the Eastern backhand grip is the one that allows you to best meet the ball with a square racquet-head alignment and with your wrist in a natural, uncontorted position.

The other one-handed-backhand-grip choice is the *Continental*, where the "V" between your thumb and index finger is directly on top of the handle. It is the same as the Continental forehand used by some players. The wrist position at impact is curled, so it is a little weaker than with the Eastern backhand.

A third option, popularized by champions Bjorn Borg, Jimmy Connors, and Chris Evert and the younger players they have inspired, is the *two-handed* backhand grip. Ideally your right hand should be in an

Two-handed backhand grip

Eastern backhand grip, although some players leave it in their forehand grip position. Place the left hand right above the right, in an Eastern forehand grip, with the palm of your left hand behind the handle. The two-handed backhand grip gives you additional stability and strength.

2. The Basic Image

As with the forehand, think of your racquet as a natural extension of your arm as the ball comes to your left side. The basic motion of the backhand is swinging your arm back and then forward to strike the ball and drive it across the net with the back of your open hand.

3. Keep Your Swing Simple

At first the backhand always seems like a more difficult shot than the forehand. But in some ways it is much simpler. From the ready position just turn completely sideways and swing your arm forward as you uncoil. Think of a swashbuckling movie star reaching over and drawing his sword out of its scabbard. Your backswing on the backhand should be a lot less elaborate than on the forehand. Much of the challenge of the shot comes from the inherently weaker grip.

4. Switch to a Backhand Grip

Turn your hand left to a backhand grip as soon as you see the ball coming on that side. You must wait in the ready position with a loose hold on the handle to make the fast adjustment.

5. Use Your Left Hand

Keep your left hand on your racquet until you finish your backswing. It helps you shift your grip, stabilizes the racquet, helps you open, close, or square up the racquet face, and enables you to make a full shoulder turn. Think of pulling the racquet back with the left hand for a fuller turn.

6. Make a Full Turn

Coil on the backswing until you are looking over your right shoulder at the ball. When you have rotated far enough so you can imagine your opponent is looking at the back of your shirt, you've made a complete turn.

Full Turn: Coil until you are looking at the ball over your right shoulder.

7. Step Forward

Trigger your forward swing by stepping forward aggressively with your right leg. Because of the less-powerful grip used on the backhand, you must transfer your weight forward and keep it there for effective shots.

8. Swing from the Shoulder

At the end of your backswing your arm should be relaxed and fairly straight. From there the forward swing should start from the shoulder, not the elbow. Elbow-leading backhands are a major cause of tennis elbow.

9. Make Contact Ahead of Your Toes

You should meet the ball farther ahead on the backhand than on the forehand. The racquet should be well in front of the toes of your right foot.

Point of Contact: Meet the ball ahead of your right foot.

10. Keep Your Head Still

Expert players talk of "staying down on the ball" as a key to a good backhand. The opposite is "pulling up" or "pulling off" the shot. One secret to staying down on the ball is to keep your head still, even after contact. Follow the ball with your eyes. But if you lift your head, the rest of your body will follow and your shot will lose its accuracy.

11. Extend Your Knuckles Forward

Your racquet head should be perpendicular to the court at impact, so the strings are facing the target. To keep them facing the target for as long as possible, think of extending your knuckles forward for as long as you can. Imagine hitting straight ahead through a half-dozen balls lined up next to each other.

12. Follow Through Out and Up

As your racquet moves toward your target on the follow-through, it also should gradually move up to lift the ball over the net. That's true for both topspin and flat backhands. Only the steepness of the upward path will vary. The one exception is on a slice, where the racquet travels down slightly through contact and into the early follow-through before rising slightly at the end.

13. Finish in a Spread-Eagle Position

Keeping your left arm back as your right arm swings forward will keep your shoulders turned and help accelerate your swing. Finish with your right arm way in front and your left arm behind, your weight on your right foot and your left foot still behind, up on its toes. A common backhand mistake is to "spin out," rotating your hips and shoulders around like a top as you swing. It inevitably pulls your back foot off the court and forward, resulting in a reverse weight shift with your body leaning backward as you hit and follow through. Finishing in a spread-eagle position will prevent that.

Spread-Eagle Finish: Keep the left arm back so you don't spin out.

The Quick Fix

1. Turn Your Grip and Body

The most common causes of an erratic backhand are a weak grip and poor preparation. You then can only poke the ball back. Like the 1960s hit song by the Byrds, the key to better backhands is "Turn, Turn, Turn." Turn your hand to the left to a full Eastern backhand grip and then turn your torso and shoulders away from the net, using your left hand to help take the racquet back as you coil. As you uncoil into the shot, keep the shoulders perpendicular to the net for as long as possible.

Correcting the Everyday Errors

1. Hitting into the Net

Aim higher. Bend your knees. Open the racquet face. Swing out toward the target. Make a higher follow-through.

2. Hitting Long

Keep your head still. Close the racquet face a little. Add some topspin. If your slice backhand is sailing long, be sure you are shifting your weight forward and aggressively following through.

3. Hitting Wide Crosscourt

Make a fuller turn. Remain sideways at impact. Swing forward toward the target, not across your body. Swing from your shoulder, not from your wrist.

4. Hitting Wide Down the Line

Turn sooner and take the racquet back earlier. Shift your weight forward. Remain sideways at impact. Make contact farther in front. Make a full forward follow-through.

Five Frequent Problems and Their Cures

1. Inadequate Strength

Use a two-handed backhand. It enables you to compensate for the inherent weakness of the one-handed grip. For many players that far outweighs several limitations. The pros of changing are increased power, leverage, and stability; greater potential for disguise; more ease hitting from an open stance. The cons of changing are restricted reach; reduced versatility; difficulty hitting a slice; trouble on low balls; more effort required in body movement; difficulty making the transition to a backhand volley; insufficient development of arm strength on backhand side. To hit a two-handed backhand, make these important adjustments.

1) Use a backhand grip with your right hand. You will have to drop your left hand from the racquet in certain emergency situations, such as wide shots. You also may choose to drop your left hand to hit with slice. In both instances you need a strong backhand grip to hit a good one-handed shot.

2) Turn so your right shoulder points toward your opponent. The turn is a little shorter than on a one-hander because your other hand is part of your grip, not just a guide.

3) Rotate your hips for power. On the one-handed backhand you should try to remain sideways for as long as possible. But on the two-hander you can generate extra power by rotating your hips rapidly into the shot while keeping your left leg behind. Think of all the photographs you've seen of Chris Evert hitting a two-hander with her skirt flaring. It was a sign of superior hip rotation.

4) Adjust your point of contact. Meet the ball somewhere between your navel and the toes of your right foot. Your left hand is in a forehand grip position, so your two-handed backhand is similar to a left-handed forehand. That means the contact point is farther back than on a one-hander.

5) Extend your left arm and hand toward your target. Use your left hand as if you are hitting a left-handed fore-hand and drive your palm out at your target. This will increase the power and depth of your shot. You sacrifice both if you pull the racquet across and around your body too soon. Players who make this mistake can hit effective crosscourt shots but are in trouble when they try to go down the line.

6) Hit on the rise. The stability of a two-handed grip and the shorter swing it necessitates make the shot ideal for hitting on the rise. Move up right to the baseline and play the ball with a slightly closed racquet face as it is bouncing up off the court. Play to a quick "bounce-hit" rhythm rather than a slower "bounce and hit" rhythm.

Two-Handed Backhand: Drive toward the target with your left hand.

2. Lack of Consistency

Rely on the slice. The slice should become your fail-safe backhand if you use one hand. It takes less energy than flat or topspin shots so it is a low-maintenance shot. The stroking motion helps the ball rise over the net. And if your basic swing is solid, you can get away with hitting late or not making a proper forward weight shift. To hit it:

1) Take the racquet back high. You must swing on a high-to-low path to impart backspin. Think of the racquet finishing at shoulder height at the end of the backswing.

2) Make a full turn. As you turn sideways with your lower body, imagine coiling your upper body so far that your back is to the net. That rotation will add pace to your shot.

3) Open the racquet face. At the end of your backswing the hitting side of the racquet strings should angle toward the sky. You should feel as if you can slice them underneath the ball from there.

Slice Backhand: Take the racquet back high with an open racquet face.

4) *Swing forward aggressively.* The slice is considered more a defensive shot than a flat or topspin backhand. The backward rotation that the motion imparts to the ball slows it down as it goes through the air. You must swing from the shoulder smoothly and with force to get depth and speed on the shot.

5) *Let the racquet face square up naturally.* As you swing forward on a downward trajectory, the strings will naturally turn into a more square position at contact. If they slide under in a completely open position, your shot will have no forward momentum.

6) *Bevel for more bite.* Try to keep the racquet face open into and after contact. Sequence photographs would show the strings nearly perpendicular to the court at impact and then tilting again after the ball has left the racquet. But that happens so fast that it is best for you to think of keeping the strings beveled throughout the swing to get the sharpest backspin. Hitting through with an open face also helps lift the ball over the net.

7) *Stop the chop.* A common cause of ineffective slices is chopping down on the ball. You must swing from high to low for a slice. But you also must swing the racquet from behind you to well in front of you. Keep your racquet moving

forward toward your target on the follow-through. If your swing ends up at your shoe tops and your underspin shot has no power and floats too high over the net, you are chopping instead of slicing.

8) *Finish in a modified spread-eagle pose.* Your racquet will rise naturally at the end of the high-to-low slice swing. As on a regular backhand, you should finish with your arms spread, the left pointing toward the back fence and the right extended toward your target. The major difference is that with the slice the racquet strings should be open to the sky, almost flat like a tray upon which you could put a drink.

9) *Set up three other shots.* The basic slice stroke is the foundation of three other backhand shots. The approach shot is a slice with a shorter backswing and a full follow-through. The volley is a slice with a very short backswing and very short follow-through. The drop shot is a slice with a full backswing and very abrupt follow-through.

3. Insufficient Topspin

Swing on a steeper low-to-high path. The racquet head should travel from around knee level at the end of the backswing to above your head and way out front at the end of the follow-through. This is achieved with a full swing, not a flick of the wrist.

1) Use your other hand. Cradling the racquet up by the head with the left hand helps you do three things: turn to a backhand grip, set the face slightly closed, and make a fuller turn.

2) Relax your elbow as you take the racquet back. It will help you generate more power at contact because your muscles can move more freely. It also will help you avoid tennis elbow.

3) Set the racquet head below the ball. In a loop preparation, you circle the racquet head up and then down on the backswing. (Use a smaller loop than on the forehand.) In a straight preparation, you drop the racquet head down as you turn back. Either way, the strings should be well below the level of the incoming ball as you start to swing

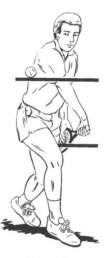

Topspin Backhand: Set the racquet below the ball at the end of the backswing.

forward. Bend your knees deeply to lower your body as you lower the racquet.

4) *Swing up and through.* You impart topspin when the strings brush up the back of the ball, but you also want to drive the ball over the net. So as you swing up, you must swing forward through the ball. Too much upward swing without enough forward swing will result in a slow, shallow shot.

5) *Keep the strings square to the target.* At impact you should be able to draw a straight line from your strings through the ball to your target. And your racquet and wrist should form a straight line parallel to the net.

6) *Finish with your racquet high and forward.* A common mistake is to break the wrist-racquet alignment by flipping the wrist over and snapping the racquet across your body right after contact. You'll generate little spin that way and you'll lose power and control. Instead, keep swinging up and forward from the shoulder without flicking your wrist.

4. Ineffective Approach Shots

Slice on the move. The backhand slice is the most widely used and effective approach shot. The simple mechanics of the stroke make it easier to hit than other shots as you move forward.

1) Check your court position. If your feet are behind the baseline, you are too deep in the court to try an approach shot in the first place.

2) Hit with slice. Think of sliding the strings under the ball as you swing from high to low. That will impart backspin on the ball so it will bounce low on your opponent's side, making the passing shot more difficult.

Approach Shot: Slide your left foot forward as you hit.

3) Shorten your backswing. You'll get extra power from your weight moving forward. And because you are inside the baseline, you don't have to hit as hard as on a full-length ground stroke.

4) Remain sideways. Your shoulders should remain parallel to the sideline until well after the ball has left the strings. That allows your racquet to follow along your target line longer, especially when approaching down the line, giving your shot better depth and accuracy.

5) Slow down but don't stop. You don't have time to pause and watch your approach shot land. You must get to the net fast. As you hit, let your left foot slide sideways toward the net behind your right foot. That will keep your body weight moving forward toward your eventual volleying position.

6) Finish out, not down. If you chop down, your shot will lack pace and depth. So follow through in front with an open racquet face.

5. High Balls

Prepare high and finish high. The high backhand is the hardest ground stroke in the game. It is difficult to get leverage on a ball that bounces around or above eye level with the inherently weaker backhand stroke. To do it:

1) Make a big shoulder turn. That will compensate for the lack of strength in your arm in such an awkward position. Don't make the common mistake of cocking the racquet back by just bendng your elbow.

2) Meet the ball farther away. When the ball is low, your arm extends down from your shoulder. When it is high, your arm extends straight out horizontally. That automatically makes the point of contact farther away from your body than on a normal backhand.

3) Aim high and end high. Your only objective with such a difficult shot is to get the ball back deep. So aim high, then swing high. The racquet head should be at ball level at the end of your back-swing, and it should remain at that height throughout the swing. Imagine the strings moving forward along a clothesline strung out just above eye level toward your target.

SERVE

SERVE

The Step-by-Step Basics

1. Take Command

When you step up to the baseline to
serve, before you even grip your racquet
you should assume the proper attitude.
The serve is the only stroke you hit
without reacting to your opponent's shot.
Everything is under your control; you are
in a position to dictate how the point
unfolds. And you have two chances—if
you miss your first serve, you have
another. So don't throw the opportunity
away. Hit every serve with a definite plan
of placement, speed, and spin. And
throughout the prestroke process and the
swing itself, be positive and relax. Tense
emotions create tense muscles that will
inhibit the smoothness and speed of your
swing.

2. Grips

The more advanced your skill level, the
more your hand should be turned toward a
full Eastern backhand grip. It will allow
you to swing the racquet around on edge
and to brush up and across the back of the

ball at impact for spin. Beginners find initial success easier to achieve by serving with a forehand grip, which will result in the strings meeting the ball face on at impact. But the serve will be a flat, pushing motion with no spin potential. So as soon as you get comfortable with the basics, turn your hand left to a Continental and, eventually, an Eastern backhand grip.

3. The Basic Image

Think of throwing your racquet up and over the net. It's an elongated motion, like a baseball pitcher winding up and hurling. Some teaching pros even have their pupils throw old racquets into the service court during lessons.

4. The Stance

Stand sideways to the net, your feet shoulder-width apart, your left foot at about a 45-degree angle to the baseline and your right foot about parallel to the baseline.

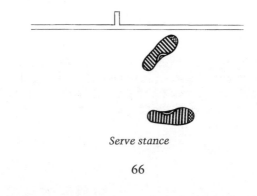

Serve stance

5. Relax Your Wrist and Grip

Your goal is a continuous, rhythmical, accelerating swing without any hitches. That requires a relaxed arm at the start of the motion. Rest the throat of the racquet across the wrist of your other arm to relax your wrist. Squeeze mostly with the thumb and index finger to relax your grip, and even then don't squeeze too tightly. In fact, to develop a loose, smooth swing, you should try hitting a few easy practice serves while holding the racquet with only your thumb and index finger.

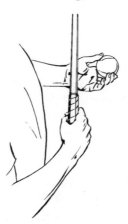

Relax Your Grip and Wrist: Rest the racquet across the wrist of your other arm and squeeze loosely. Hold the ball gently in your fingertips.

6. Start Slowly, Then Accelerate

The strings should meet the ball just as the racquet head is reaching its maximum speed. You've got to give yourself enough time during the service swing for all of the mechanical elements to come together at that optimum moment. The way to do that is to slow down your swing. Begin with a slow, rhythmical backswing, letting the racquet head accelerate naturally as you swing it down, around, and up to meet the ball.

7. Move Your Arms Together

You can initiate the service swing by letting both arms drop together slowly from the ready position toward your front knee. Let gravity be your helper. As your arms start down, begin coiling by turning your hips, trunk, and shoulders away from the net. Let both arms move together naturally as you coil. Think of the coiling action as loading up a spring that will release its energy in an upward, outward bound. Your arms should separate around the bottom of the backswing arc, with the tossing arm starting up and forward as the racquet arm starts up and back.

8. Use a Loop Backswing

The serve backswing is a looping action in which the racquet moves down, around, and up. One way of facilitating that loop is to visualize your palm facing down at the point when your racquet is extended farthest behind you on the backswing.

Loop Backswing: As you swing the racquet up, lift your tossing arm.

9. Release the Ball

As your racquet starts rising up behind your head from that palm-down position during the final part of the loop, your left arm should begin to rise, too, out front and to your right. When your left hand reaches about eye level, you should open your fingers to release the ball. At the end of the backswing, your racquet should be cocked behind your head, the ball should be up and out in front and your left arm should still be extended toward it. If you let the ball fall without hitting it, it should land well in front of the baseline. Tossing forward gets all your weight moving forward into the serve.

10. Transfer Your Weight

Your weight should shift during the serve like a rocking chair. Although some players begin with their weight already on the back foot, you can build better rhythm by starting with your weight slightly on your front foot. As you coil and swing the racquet back and up, your weight should shift onto your back foot in rhythm with your swing. Then as you swing forward into impact, your weight should rock forward toward the target.

11. Extend at Impact

Throw your racquet up and out at the ball from behind your head to make contact. Let your shoulders, trunk, and hips uncoil, channeling into your arm all the energy you've stored by coiling on the backswing. Your racquet head should move like the end of a whip. At impact your body should be leaning forward in a straight line from your toes to the tip of your racquet like a launching missile for maximum leverage on the serve.

Extend on Impact: Lean forward in a straight line from toes to racquet tip.

12. Hit Up, Snap Down

You must hit up on the ball for your serve to clear the net. You also must accelerate the wrist to get maximum racquet head speed. The way to do that is think, "Hit up, snap down." Your wrist doesn't actually snap over (if it did, you'd hit the ball down into the court in front of you). What happens is that your wrist and forearm pronate. During pronation, your palm turns from facing the left sideline to facing forward or even a little toward the right sideline. As it does, the racquet, which has been moving forward on edge with the hitting side of the strings facing the left sideline, squares up to the ball at impact and then turns out, so the strings are facing the right sideline. It's a subtle but critical move. If you use an Eastern backhand or Continental grip, pronation should occur naturally. A relaxed wrist is imperative here. The looser your wrist, the faster you can snap it and the more power and spin you'll get.

Hit Up, Snap Down: Let your arm naturally pronate so your palm turns from left to right.

13. Keep Your Head and Eyes Up

Just as you should extend your body up, so too should you keep your head up throughout the entire serve. If you drop your head, you'll pull your body down and your serve will go into the net. Think "Chin up at contact."

14. Step Forward into the Court

If you've hit the ball properly out front and shifted your weight into the shot, your momentum should make you naturally step forward into the court as your racquet follows through down and across in front of your body. Even if you don't intend to rush the net behind your serve, take that big forward step. Any attempt to inhibit it will prevent you from getting all your weight into the shot, and you will sacrifice power.

S
E
R
V
E

15. Count "1-2-3" for Better Timing

If you have trouble coordinating the simultaneous movement of your racquet and tossing arms, try counting to three as you serve. On beat 1, both arms go down and around. On beat 2, the arms separate and both go up, with the right lifting the racquet behind your head and the left lifting the ball into the air to your front and right. On beat 3 the racquet swings forward and hits the ball. A "1-2-3" rhythm will result in a smoother, more synchronized service swing.

The Quick Fix

1. Droop Your Wrist

You don't have to muscle the ball to serve hard. In fact, trying to swing really hard usually inhibits your serve. You do, however, need to swing loosely so the racquet can accelerate during the motion. And to do that your arm and wrist must be loose. When your swing starts feeling tight and constricted, begin your motion by drooping your wrist. As you rest your racquet over your ball-tossing arm in the ready position, let your wrist go totally limp. Let the racquet head dangle almost to where it's pointing down at the court. That will help your arm stay tension-free throughout the swing.

2. Think "Head Up, Hit Up"

Your first job is to get the serve across the net. Then comes the task of hitting it in. When you start hitting the net, it is likely you are dropping your head,which is causing you to hit down. So remind yourself on every serve to keep your head up and to hit up.

Correcting the Everyday Errors

1. Hitting into the Net

Toss higher. Keep your head up and hit up.

2. Hitting Long

Toss farther in front. Shift your weight forward. Add some spin. Snap your wrist.

3. Hitting Wide Left

Make a full coil. Pronate your wrist. Swing up and out, not across.

4. Hitting Wide Right

Toss farther in front. Shift your weight forward. Add some slice.

Four Frequent Problems and Their Cures

1. Inconsistent Toss

S
E
R
V
E

Lift it, don't throw it. A tennis ball weighs about two ounces. It doesn't take much strength to toss it into the right place on the serve. Use a lifting action instead of a throwing action. Here's how to make your toss more consistent and accurate.

1) Hold the ball in your fingertips. Grip the ball extremely lightly between your thumb and first three fingertips. It should not touch any part of your palm. And it should be held so lightly that there would be virtually no resistance if another person pulled it out of your hand.

2) Keep the palm sideways. As you move your tossing arm down and back up, your palm should face the right sideline most of the time. If you turn the palm up at the sky, it will result in too much tension in your tossing arm, which can affect control.

3) Raise the tossing arm from the shoulder. Keep your wrist and elbow joints relatively quiet during the toss. Lift your arm from the shoulder joint, keeping the arm relaxed but basically straight, to keep your toss under control.

4) Try two balls to quiet the wrist. Your toss will go out of control if you flick the ball up with your wrist. If you have that problem, serve holding two balls. It should reduce or eliminate excess wrist action.

5) Open your fingers to let the ball go. The ball should leave your hand as the hand reaches forehead height. Just open your fingers and let the ball go. It is a gentle releasing action. Any extra movement in the fingers, hand, or wrist will make the toss go off-line. The momentum of your arm moving up should be all the energy you need to put the ball in the right place. Make sure your arm keeps moving up even after the ball is gone, the same way your racquet follows through toward the target on a ground stroke.

6) Toss with your weight back. By the time you release the ball, your weight should have shifted almost entirely onto your back foot. If you toss as you are still rocking back, chances are the toss will sail back over your head.

7) Toss up a chimney. If you actually traced the path of a perfect toss, it would arc in a steep parabola going up behind the baseline and falling a foot or so in front of it. But if you are plagued by a persistently crooked toss, visualize tossing the ball up the inside of a chimney without it hitting the walls.

8) Toss only as high as your swing can reach. Your goal on the serve is to make a smooth, continuous swing. One way to do that is to toss the ball only as high as you can reach at full extension, so you hit the ball at its apex. If you toss too high, you may have to decelerate your swing, creating a hitch as you wait for the ball to drop into the hitting zone. Moreover, hitting a falling ball is harder than hitting one that is cresting because the falling ball is moving faster through the hitting zone. If your toss is too high, you may be using excess wrist action in your release or you may simply be lifting your tossing arm too aggressively from the shoulder.

Conversely, a low toss will force you to rush your swing and will prevent you from hitting at full extension. If your toss is too low, be a little more aggressive with your lifting action and make sure your tossing arm keeps rising to full stretch after the ball has left your hand.

9) *Let a bad toss fall unhit.* There's no rule that says you must swing at a bad toss. Indeed, if your toss is off-line, too high or too low, let it fall to the court unstruck and begin again. It is a fault, however, if you swing at the ball and whiff it.

2. Insufficient Spin

Adjust your grip, toss, and swing path. Good players hit almost all serves, even flat ones, with some spin. The three basic types of serves are flat, slice, and topspin.

Grip for Spin

Use a full Eastern backhand grip. It will enable you to brush the strings across the back of the ball to impart the proper rotation as you swing up and forward through impact.

Toss Locations for Spin

Ideally you should hit all types of serves off the same type of toss to disguise your intentions from your opponent. In reality, you can make it easier to hit the three different kinds of serves by positioning your toss in different places. Visualizing a clock face on the court helps. Think that the top of your head is the center of the clock as you are poised to strike the ball.

Toss locations: Toss at 1 o'clock for a normal serve, at 12 o'clock for topspin, and at 2 o'clock for a slice.

For a flat serve, toss the ball at 1 o'clock. That will enable you to hit right through the back of the ball. For a slice serve, toss the ball at 2 o'clock. That will enable you to brush sideways across the back of the ball. And for a topspin serve, toss the ball at 12 o'clock. That will enable you to brush up the back of the ball.

Thinking of the top of your head as the center of the clock face also should encourage you to toss the ball properly forward into the court regardless of the type of spin you use.

Swing Paths for Spin

The path of the racquet at impact determines the type of spin. The easiest way to understand those swing paths is to visualize of the back of the ball as the face of a clock.

For a flat serve, the strings should move right through the center of the clockface as you swing up and forward. A flat serve has a lot of pace but a low margin of safety because of its low trajectory over the net and lack of spin to pull the ball down into the court.

For a slice serve, the strings should brush sideways across the back of the ball from 9 o'clock to 3 o'clock as you swing up and forward. That will impart a sideways rotation that makes the ball bounce low and to your opponent's right. The slice serve has more safety than a flat one and should be your bread-and-butter delivery.

For a topspin serve, the strings should brush up across the back of the ball from about 7 o'clock to about 1 o'clock as you swing up and forward. That will impart a forward rotation that makes the ball kick up high and slightly to your opponent's left. The topspin serve is the most difficult to hit, but it has the greatest margin of safety because the upward forward rotation makes the ball clear the net by a good margin and then pulls it down into the court.

Swing Paths: For a slice serve, brush from 9 o'clock to 3 o'clock. For topspin, brush from 7 o'clock to 1 o'clock. For a flat serve, hit straight through from the center of the clock to 12 o'clock.

3. Insufficient Power

Use your body. A smooth, continuous swing with a loose forearm and wrist are the building blocks of more power. But you trigger speed in your arm with your bigger body parts.

1) Bend your knees. This will result in a greater thrust up and forward into the ball. The uncoiling into the shot begins from the ground up. As you spring up at the ball from the knees, it triggers a chain reaction of forward rotation from your upper body, unleashing the whipping action of your arm.

2) Turn the shoulders. The more you coil during the backswing, the more energy you will release through your arm as you uncoil into your forward swing. The resulting increase in racquet head speed will give you more power.

3) Lean into the shot. At contact your body should look like the Leaning Tower of Pisa. A straight line leaning into the court should be formed from the position of the toes to the racquet tip. That indicates you are getting maximum forward momentum and maximum leverage on the serve, which should translate into maximum power.

4. Too Many Double Faults

Spin the second serve aggressively.
Double faults seem preventable because
you have two chances to get your serve in.
But bad technique, psychological pressure,
or both can afflict even the game's greatest
and lead to double faults. A reliable second
serve hit with sufficient spin to give you a
large margin of safety over the net is the
best preventative. Some further specifics:

1) Get the first serve in. You may be
putting too much pressure on your
second serve by missing a majority of
first serves. Take some pace off the first
ball and hit it with more spin to increase
your percentage.

2) Hit with topspin. Toss the ball
straight ahead instead of to your right,
then brush the strings up the back of the
ball from 7 o'clock to 1 o'clock as you
swing up and out. That will impart a
forward, upward rotation that will arc
the ball higher over the net and then
bring it down on the other side. It's the
safest way to hit a second serve. The
second best choice is a slice, with the
toss forward and out to the right and a 9
o'clock to 3 o'clock brushing action at
impact as you swing up and out. A slice
second serve won't have as much net

clearance as a topspin, but the spin will give you a greater safety margin than a flat serve. Regardless of which spin you use, think of hitting up to get the ball over the net. More missed second serves hit the net, especially on pressure points, than sail long or wide.

3) *Swing aggressively.* You should swing as hard at your spin second serve as you do at your flat first one. Because you are brushing the back of the ball instead of hitting straight through it, you still have a safety margin. In fact, the faster the brushing action the more spin you impart. Swinging hard also will help your nerves. If you slow your swing down and try to steer the serve, it won't go in when the pressure is on. Or if it does, it won't have much pace or spin on it.

4) *Prepare mentally.* Before you even start your second serve swing, you've got to counteract the psychological pressure of the situation. First, think positively. If you think about missing, you probably will. Instead, visualize the ball landing successfully in your opponent's service court. As server, you are still in control. So approach the second serve with the idea that you are the player dictating the play. Second, have a plan. Decide where your second serve is going, how hard you are going to hit it, and with how much

spin. Then stick to it. When you step up to the line, just think "execute." Third, take your time. Too many players rush right into the second serve after missing the first. Instead, adopt a pre-swing routine: Take your position at the baseline, bounce the ball a specific number of times, take a deep breath, and then serve. Do the exact same thing before every first and second serve until it becomes a semiconscious ritual.

RETURN OF SERVE

The Step-by-Step Basics

1. Stand Tall

The return ready position is similar to the baseline ready position. Your weight should be on the balls of your feet and your knees should be slightly flexed. Your racquet head should be pointing almost straight out at your opponent, rather than cocked up above the wrist, unless you are playing an opponent with a high-kicking topspin serve. Avoid crouching way down or bending forward from the waist. If you are too low you cannot move fast sideways because you have to straighten up first. It's better to keep your upper body aligned over the balls of your feet for good balance. On the other hand, don't stand as erect as a statue.

2. Watch the Toss, Not the Racquet

Focus on the ball even before it leaves your opponent's hand. A toss to your right-handed opponent's right usually means a slice serve is coming. A toss ahead of the right shoulder usually means a flat serve. And a toss over thc head or farther left usually means a topspin kicker. If you watch your opponent's racquet swinging up into the ball, you might lose track of the ball, and you might flinch unnecessarily if the swing is exceptionally hard. Play the ball, not the swing.

3. Move Your Feet with the Toss

Even though some pros do it, there's no need to shuffle your feet like a disco dancer while in the ready position. But you must get your feet moving during the toss. Flatfootedness is usually fatal on the return. Experienced players take an almost imperceptible hop just before their opponents make contact with the ball. That sets their feet in motion for a big move right or left. A more aggressive method, assuming you are reading your opponent's serve well, is to stand back and take a big step forward as the server hits, like an infielder charging a ground ball. You may get beaten badly if you make a bad read, but most times you'll hit a sharper return.

4. Turn Your Shoulders First

As soon as you recognize which side the ball is coming on, rotate your shoulders. That may be all the backswing you'll have time to make on a fast serve.

5. Shorten Your Backswing

Beyond the shoulder turn, keep your preparation compact. Make only a short backswing with your arm. Good timing is critical to a solid return, and the longer your backswing the more chance you have of mistiming the shot. If you meet the ball squarely, and the compact stroke will increase the likelihood of meeting the ball squarely, your opponent's pace should make up for the swing speed you sacrifice with the compact stroke.

6. Lean in if You Can't Step In

Ideally you'll have time to step into the return like you do on a normal ground stroke. But sometimes the ball is moving too fast to do so or you simply get a late jump tracking it. When that happens, try to lean in as you hit. Use your body weight as a brace against your opponent's pace.

7. Squeeze at Contact

Speed and spin on your opponent's serve, together or individually, can knock your racquet head off the target line, so hold the racquet very firmly at impact.

8. Keep the Strings Square to Your Target

The return is first of all a control shot. The way to ensure that control is to keep the strings on line with your target prior to, during, and after contact. Imagine that the strings of your racquet have a manufacturer's logo stenciled on them like the pros' racquets do. As you swing your racquet into impact and then follow through, that logo should be clearly visible to your opponent.

The Quick Fix

1. Block It Back

A full swing on the return is great when it works, but it often doesn't work. You simply don't have enough time. If your returns are erratic, approach the problem from the other end of the stroking spectrum and just block the ball back, almost like hitting a volley. Just stick the racquet out in front of the oncoming ball with no backswing, shift your weight forward, and squeeze the handle tight. Let the pace of the serve become the pace on your return.

Correcting the Everyday Errors

1. Hitting into the Net

Aim higher. Open the racquet face. Squeeze tight at contact.

2. Hitting Long

Shorten your backswing. Shift your weight forward. Close the racquet face.

3. Hitting Wide

Turn your shoulders sooner. Shift your weight forward. Squeeze tight at contact. Aim over the center net strap for safety. Keep the racquet strings facing forward.

Five Frequent Problems and Their Cures

1. Fast, Flat Serves

Use an open stance. Some serves don't allow you time to turn and step with your lower body. So hit with your feet aligned parallel with the net. In fact, returning a hard serve is the one time when an open-stance backhand makes sense. It's especially useful when that serve is a jammer aimed right at your body, because the way to hit that shot is with a backhand pulling the racquet across in front of your hips. Unless it's a jammer, though, when you use an open stance on either the forehand

or backhand return you still must turn
your shoulders.

*Open-Stance Return: Use it to return a fast,
flat serve to the backhand.*

2. Wide Slice Serves

Move in diagonally. If you move straight
sideways, either the ball will hit the fence
before you reach it or you'll be so far out of
court by the time you hit it you'll be out of
the point as well. So step forward to cut
down the angle as you step across.

3. High-Bouncing Kick Serves

Take the ball on the rise. Most topspin
serves are aimed at your backhand, and the
high backhand is a difficult shot. So don't
let the ball get up there. As soon as you see

the arcing trajectory of a kick serve, step forward. Then take a short backswing and hit straight through the rising ball with a firm grip so the spin doesn't knock the strings off-line. If the ball gets up on you a little anyway, make your backhand a short-swing slice or chip return.

4. Second Serves

Move inside the baseline. Some players get lulled into passive carelessness returning of second serves because they know second serves are likely to be slower than first serves. Instead, that's the time to be more aggressive. Begin by stepping inside the baseline to take your ready position. Then step forward into the shot. You'll be in the same position as you would be hitting an approach shot, so consider following your return to the net if it's a good one. Another payoff of moving forward to return a second serve is that you'll put added pressure on your opponent. When he sees you crowding him, he may overhit the second serve and double fault.

5. A Service Onslaught

Shift your receiving positions. When you feel your opponent is serving you off the court, your best chance at ending the barrage is to break up his rhythm. You could stall between points, but that's gamesmanship bordering on cheating. (The rules specifically state that the receiver must play to the reasonable pace of the server; tournament players are allowed a maximum of 25 seconds between points.) Instead, show your opponent different looks by varying your receiving position. The rules say you can stand anywhere (even inside the service court if you want to be that foolish). Back up, move to the extreme left to run around your backhand, or even move in and crowd the service line. This last may be considered gamesmanship, but it is permitted. If your opponent notices what you are doing, he may start to think too much and lose his service flow.

NET PLAY

VOLLEY

The Step-by-Step Basics

1. Grips

Use the Continental, halfway between
the Eastern forehand and Eastern backhand
with the "V" between your thumb and
index finger at the center of the top of the
handle. It allows you to hit either a forehand or backhand volley without changing
grips, which is essential in fast-paced net
play. A forehand grip results in a racquet
face that is too open on backhand volleys,
which then lack power and penetration. A
backhand grip makes it difficult to meet
forehand volleys out in front, inhibiting
your ability to hit them down the line, and
it may promote excessive use of the wrist.

2. The Basic Image

Think of holding your racquet out ahead
of you to block the ball's flight with the
strings as it comes over the net. The volley
should be a no-frills stroke.

3. The Ready Position

The only change from the baseline ready position (see FOREHAND, p.31) is that you should wait with the racquet head up higher. That will help you *keep* the racquet head up on volleys. If you find you're reacting slow at the net, you might also wait with your elbows a little farther out in front. But don't extend them out so far you end up volleying with a straight racquet arm.

Net Ready Position: Wait with the racquet head at eye level, higher than at the baseline.

4. Set Your Wrist

The first move on the volley from the hands out front ready position is the key to the whole stroke. On the forehand side, lay back your wrist as if catching a ball. That will square the strings up with the approaching ball. *Maintain that wrist-racquet angle throughout the whole stroke.* If it breaks down, the racquet head will move ahead of the wrist and you will lose control. Setting the racquet for the backhand volley is simpler. Using your left hand as it cradles the throat, just turn the racquet to the side so the strings are square to the approaching ball. Then, as on the fore-hand, don't let the racquet head move ahead of the wrist at any time during the stroke.

Set Your Wrist: Bend your wrist as if catching a ball on the forehand volley.

5. Use Your Eyes

Keeping your eye on the ball is so funda-mental it is hardly worth mentioning on most shots. But it is particularly important on the volley because the ball is moving so fast and the exchange of shots is so rapid. Instead of thinking of bending your knees, try to keep your eyes at the same level as the approaching ball. If you mis-hit a lot of volleys, it may be due to not watching the ball closely enough.

6. Turn Your Shoulders

After you turn your racquet square to the ball, turn your shoulders. That move will take the racquet back as far as it should go. You should use virtually no arm backswing on the volley. The racquet head should never go back beyond your rear shoulder (the right on a forehand, the left on a back-hand). The only exception is on a very slow high ball when you have ample time.

7. Step Forward

The volley is an offensive shot, and you should attack the ball with your feet as well as your arm. So step forward aggressively into the volley whenever you have time. Once you have set the racquet it will move forward at the same speed as the forward momentum of your body, even without a swing. Go out after the ball; don't wait for it to come to you.

Forehand Volley: Step forward and make contact in front while maintaining the racquet and wrist angle.

8. Make Contact in Front

The forward swing of the volley should be a punching action as your shoulders uncoil. On the backhand, separate your hands, with the left hand going back, to initiate the forward stroke. Meet the ball well in front of you, ahead of where you set the racquet in the first place. Squeeze tight at impact to keep the strings on line.

9. Lead with the Lower Edge

Except on high volleys, it's a good idea to hit with a little underspin for control. To do that, tilt the racquet head so the bottom edge is slightly ahead and the face is barely open. Avoid twisting your wrist to flip the racquet under the ball or to chop down sharply, or you'll lose control and pace.

10. Follow Through Forward

On the forehand, push your palm and racquet head forward at the target as a unit. On the backhand, push your knuckles and racquet head forward at the target as a unit. On both, keep your wrist and racquet in line. That's how you get depth and accuracy.

Backhand Volley: Drive the racquet strings forward by pushing your knuckles forward.

97

The Quick Fix

1. Set and Step

The number one cause of inconsistent volleys is swinging at the shot in a mistaken quest for power. All you need to do is set the racquet square to the ball and step forward to hit it. If your wrist and racquet are properly aligned at contact and your grip is firm, the pace of your opponent's shot will provide you with all the power you need. To eliminate over-swinging, practice volleying while standing with your back against a fence. Drill until you can make solid contact time after time without your racquet hitting the fence behind you.

Correcting the Everyday Errors

1. Hitting into the Net

Open the racquet face. Get your eyes down to the level of the ball. Make contact farther in front.

2. Hitting Long

Turn your shoulders sideways. Block, don't swing. Make contact farther in front. Keep your wrist laid back and firm.

3. Hitting Wide

Turn your shoulders. Eliminate any backswing. Keep the wrist and racquet aligned at contact. Push forward, not across, so the strings stay facing the target.

Six Frequent Problems and Their Cures

1. High Volleys

Set the racquet high. The strings should not only be square to the ball, but also at the same height as the ball. Make sure you turn your shoulders. Keep your eyes intently focused on the ball, then meet it out front with a firm wrist. If the oncoming shot is a high floater, you can extend your compact backswing. But the shoulder turn is imperative. If you don't coil, you'll swing across instead of forward and hit the ball out.

2. Low Volleys

Get your head and hand low. The tendency on low volleys is to stick the racquet head down without lowering your body. You then lose the wrist-racquet angle. Try to get your head and hand down as close to the level of the ball as possible. That will make you bend your knees and keep your wrist in the proper alignment.

Then reach out to make contact as far forward as possible and open the racquet face more than normal for safe net clearance.

3. Jammers

Hit a backhand. The way to volley a hard-hit ball that is aimed right at your belly is to use your backhand volley. Draw the racquet across your stomach and hold on tight. If you try to return the ball with a forehand volley, you won't be able to keep the racquet in front of you and you'll be handcuffed. If that hard-hit shot is coming at head level, duck. It's not worth risking a serious injury trying to hit it. Moreover, a ball hit that hard that high may fly long.

4. Wobbly Racquet Head

Choke up. Some players find it difficult to keep the racquet head steady on volleys. For better control, choke up on the handle a little, like a baseball player choking up on the bat. You'll trade a little reach for a lot more consistency. Even world-class pro Zina Garrison does it.

5. Putting the Ball Away

Close in on the net. If you've worked the point properly, the volley eventually should be a finishing shot. The percentage play is to hit your first volley deep to the corner, then angle the second volley cross-court to the opposite side "T"where the service line and sideline intersect. To make that angle, though, you must hit the second volley close to the net. So move forward aggressively. Also, concentrate on aiming for a spot on the court instead of paying too much attention to your opponent. If you watch him out of the corner of your eye and worry about him reaching your put-away, you'll overhit and miss the shot, and that may cause you to play the next put-away opportunity too cautiously.

6. Half -Volleys

Use the racquet as a wall. The half-volley—tennis's short-hop shot—is an essential element of any net player's arsenal. Visualize your racquet strings as a wall that the ball ricochets off of after skipping off the court. All you want to do is get the ball back deep so you can move in closer to the net to hit the next ball on the fly. Here's how to do it:

1) Get down low. You should bend your knees so that when you make contact your racquet and hand are on the same horizontal plane. The common tendency is to just stick the racquet straight down and try to scoop the ball over the net. The result usually is an error or a weak, shallow shot that sets your opponent up for the passing shot.

Half-Volley: Bend your knees so your racquet and hand are on the same level, then hood the racquet face.

2) Reach forward. You have no time for a backswing. Set the racquet as far in front as you can reach and hold it steady with a firm grip.

3) Close the face. As the ball bounces sharply off the court, it will tend to shoot off your strings at a similarly sharp upward angle. You can control the shot better by slightly hooding the racquet face at impact.

4) Keep moving forward. Let your forward momentum act as your follow-through. It will enhance the depth of your shot.

5) Hit to your opponent's weaker side. The half-volley is a defensive shot. Your opponent has forced you to hit up. Your job is to stay in the point and stay out of trouble. So aim the half-volley deep to your opponent's weaker ground stroke and move forward to a more offensive net position. The mechanics of the shot are hard enough. There's no payoff in considering any other placement options.

OVERHEAD

The Step-by-Step Basics

1. The Basic Image

Imagine hammering the ball like a nail. You are driving the nail into a wall stud above your head. The nail is long and the wood is hard. So you want to whack it. The same applies to overhead. The ball is high, you are close to the net, and the shot should end the point. So smash it.

2. Turn Sideways

As soon as you see that your opponent has hit a lob, turn sideways to the net.

That not only puts you in proper position to make a good swing, it also puts you in the right position to back up fast.

Overhead: Turn sideways, track the ball with your left arm, and keep your head up.

3. Cock the Racquet Back and Up

As you turn, raise the racquet up behind your head. If you take the racquet down, around, and up, as though serving the overhead, you'll risk mistiming the shot—and will most likely hit the ball late, after it has fallen too low. On the serve, you hit the ball at the apex of the toss, when it is almost still. On the overhead, you hit the ball as it is falling from the sky at a much faster speed. That's a much harder job.

4. Track with Your Left Arm

At the same time you raise the racquet with your right arm, raise your left arm and point your hand or even an extended index finger at the ball. Line up that hand as if you were going to catch the ball. Your left hand will thus serve as your radar, guiding your eyes to the ball as it falls. On a bright day, you can also use your left hand to shade your eyes from the sun.

5. Two Ways to Retreat

When the lob is short, you can retreat by backpedaling with a shuffle step—your feet come together and separate with each step, but your right leg is always the farther from the net. When the lob is deeper, though, it is better to use crossover steps and actually run back under the ball. However, if you haven't turned sideways in the first place, you'll quickly get out of balance as you backpedal.

6. Point of Contact

Swing up and out so you meet the ball in front of your body with your right shoulder and your arm at full extension. Keep your head up and your eyes on the ball into the follow-through. Pulling your head down will result in a miss. Snap your wrist for power. Unless the ball has sailed a bit behind your head and you need the extra control you get with some spin, hit the overhead flat. You'll never have a better angle for smashing the ball down hard into your opponent's court, so go for it.

7. Shift Your Weight Forward

As you swing up and out, push off your back leg to transfer your weight forward. The ball often will sail long if you smash it with your weight moving backward. Finally, move back into the net after you smash the ball. If it ball comes back, chances are it will be a shallower lob that you can clobber if you're at the net waiting for it.

The Quick Fix

1. Ready, Aim, Fire

More overheads are missed because the player doesn't prepare for them properly than for any other reason. Get ready immediately by turning and taking the racquet back. It should be an instantaneous reaction to any lob. Then take aim by homing in on the ball with your left hand and eyes. Last, fire away with an aggressive swing, keeping your head up until your heavy artillery is long on its way toward enemy territory.

Correcting the Everyday Errors

1. Hitting into the Net

Watch the ball closely. Keep your head and nonracquet arm up. Reach up to meet the ball.

2. Hitting Long

Take the racquet straight back, not down and around. Keep your head and other arm up. Reach up to meet the ball. Shift your weight forward. Snap your wrist.

3. Hitting Wide

Aim down the middle; the overhead will be hard enough to return.

Four Frequent Problems and Their Cures

1. High, Short Lobs

Smash off the bounce. It is extremely difficult to properly time the overhead for solid contact off skyscraper lobs. Other lobs are too high and deep to reach with a jump overhead. So use a bounce overhead. Move back fast so you can set up well behind the spot where the ball lands. Why? First, it is always easier to hit an overhead moving forward into the shot than moving backward. Second, laws of physics dictate that a ball will bounce up at the same angle it falls. That means it is going to carry well past the point at which it strikes the court. If you set up there, the ball may bounce out of your reach by going over your head.

2. High, Deep Lobs

Jump. The leaping overhead may be the game's most spectacular shot. Push off your right leg and allow it to swing forward in a scissors kick as you land on your left leg. Jumping does two things: it gives you greater vertical reach and it enables you to shift your weight into the shot, albeit on more of an upward than forward thrust, which is still preferable to hitting while your weight is moving backward.

3. Low, Deep Lobs

Use a skyhook. Well-disguised offensive lobs don't give you enough time to set up and swing with a regular overhead. You've got to improvise to reach a ball that may already be behind your head. Try the Jimmy Connors skyhook. Extend your racquet behind you with a straight arm. Then swing up and forward with a windmill action, making contact as high as you can behind your head. Keep your extended arm moving forward in a full follow-through.

4. Lobs over the Backhand

Hit a backhand overhead. You don't have a lot of strength high over your backhand side, so avoid getting fancy with this shot. Turn sideways and take your racquet back by extending your arm out almost straight, but relaxed, from the shoulder. Then swing it up and forward in almost the same kind of windmill action you use on a skyhook. On this shot, though, make contact above and in front of your head instead of behind it. Keep your head and eyes up as you follow through forward and high. Elite players add snap to the shot by cocking the racquet head back with their wrists and snapping it through the ball at impact. It is safer, though, not to take the racquet head past the point of its being parallel with the court on the backswing, and to swing forward with a relatively quiet wrist. Otherwise, you may mistime the ball and hit it late.

LOB

The Step-by-Step Basics

1. The Basic Image

Drive the ball into the sky. In other words, think of the lob as a full ground stroke that you hit vertically instead of horizontally.

2. Defensive Lob

This high, deep lob, hit flat, has two purposes. The first is to buy you some time to get back into position when your opponent has pulled you out of court. The second is to back an aggressive opponent off the net. Use a full backswing that ends below the oncoming ball. Open the face as you swing forward and up into impact, and accelerate the racquet head through the hitting zone. Finish with a long, high follow-through. If the lob indeed clears your opponent's head before he can hit an overhead, forcing him to turn around and run the ball down, advance to the net yourself. Chances are his reply will be a lob, and you'll then be in position to smash it away.

3. Offensive Lob

This low, rapidly rising lob can be used as a third passing-shot option (the two basics are crosscourt and down-the-line ground strokes) or as a way of backing a net-hugging opponent off the net.

The more common offensive lob is a topspin. Use the same preparation you use on a topspin ground stroke (usually a looping backswing with a closed racquet face). Then swing up aggressively on a low-to-high path so you brush hard up the back of the ball to impart the spin. Finish the low-to-high forward swing higher than you do on a topspin ground stroke, but make sure you swing forward enough to give the lob the necessary depth to clear your opponent. Your racquet head should follow an upward path like a car climbing the ramp of a roller-coaster. If you do it right, the ball will climb up just over your opponent's head, then plunge down on the other side and bounce out of reach.

The other offensive lob option is the low slice backhand lob, what the pros sometimes call a teaser. Prepare like you are hitting a slice backhand ground stroke, but keep the racquet face almost wide open at contact and accelerate on an upward path rather than on the high-to-low swing path of a slice ground stroke. Aim the shot over your opponent's backhand side; if the ball doesn't get all the way over him, he'll at least be faced with a difficult backhand overhead.

The Quick Fix

1. Aim for the Clouds

Far more points are lost on lobs that are too short and too low than on lobs that are long. And the only time you can lose the point by hitting a lob too high is when you are playing indoors and the ball strikes the ceiling. So if your lobs are erratic, play it safe with this underrated shot and really sky the ball.

Correcting the Everyday Errors

1. Hitting Long

Open the racquet face more. Hit on a steeper trajectory.

2. Hitting Wide

Aim down the middle. It's a bail-out shot, so make it as safe as possible.

Three Frequent Problems and Their Cures

1. Insufficient Height and/or Depth

Finish with your hand above your head. On all ground strokes, one key to accuracy is to drive your hand toward the target, and on a lob, your target is high in the air. If the ball goes high enough but not deep enough, close the racquet face a little or flatten the arc of your swing a little.

2. Ineffective Defensive Lobs When Retreating

Hit extra hard. When your opponent's lob gets over your head and you have to run behind your baseline to return it, the safe play is to hit a high lob of your own in return. Run back on a line parallel to the ball's flight. That way you'll be able to make a full, uncramped swing when you reach it. And you'll need that full swing, because all of your momentum is heading away from your opponent's court. You've got to really smack the ball to drive it high and deep into your opponent's court. Make sure you finish with a long, high follow-through.

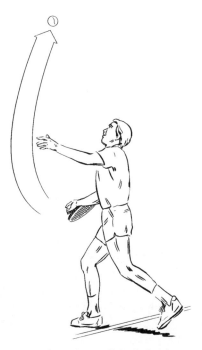

Retreating Lob: Make a full, high-finishing swing to drive the ball back deep.

3. Insufficient Disguise on Topspin Lobs

Hit with your weight forward. Surprise is a big factor in the success of a topspin lob. A lot of players can hide their intentions on the backswing, but they give the shot away at the last moment by leaning back just before contact. Work on hitting the topspin lob with your weight on your front foot.

TOUCH SHOTS

The Step-by-Step Basics

1. The Basic Image

Think of your strings as a pillow. Touch shots—the drop shot, the drop volley, and the lob volley—are the ultimate change-of-pace shots. You want to manipulate the racquet in such a way that the strings take all the pace out of your opponent's shot and return the ball with delicate finesse. It's an art to be able to return a hard-hit ball with a softly hit one.

2. Drop Shot

Because it's a slice shot, most players hit a drop shot more often off the backhand. You should be at least a yard inside the baseline and your opponent should be behind his baseline when you attempt a drop shot. Use the same open-face preparation you use on a slice ground stroke. As you swing from high to low into impact, relax your grip and abbreviate your follow-through. The ball should pop off the strings in a minilob trajectory, rise safely over the net, and fall softly in your opponent's fore-court. A good drop shot should bounce a few times before it reaches your oppo-nent's service line. It's the tennis equiv-alent of a bunt in baseball. Don't get cute and attempt to snap the strings sharply under the ball to apply heavy backspin; it's too easy to err. Move in behind the shot a few steps, directly in front of your opponent, to cut off his angle of reply.

Drop Shot: Hit a soft slice backhand with a relaxed grip and abbreviated follow-through.

3. Drop Volley

Set your racquet face forward and square to the ball as you do on a normal volley. Open the face and loosen your grip at contact. Let the racquet head fall back from the impact of the ball as if you were catching an egg.

4. Lob Volley

Used principally in doubles when all four players are at the net, the lob volley is the net equivalent of the offensive lob: its success depends largely on surprise. Prepare as if you are going to hit a regular volley. Then, just before impact, open the face wide and push the ball up and over your opponent's head. Make enough of a firm, upward follow-through to ensure you won't be facing a point-blank overhead.

The Quick Fix

1. Use Soft Hands

If you can't get any touch on your shots, you probably are squeezing the handle too tightly. At contact, squeeze only as hard as you must to keep the racquet head from twisting, then relax your grip as you feel the ball leaving the strings. Let your hand and forearm act as a shock absorber to take the pace off the ball. If you play with a death grip on the racquet at all times—what some experts refer to as hard hands—not only will you sacrifice touch, but you'll risk arm fatigue, too.

One Frequent Problem and Its Cure

1. Insufficient Touch

Do two drills. Some players, John McEnroe being the paramount example, naturally have a better touch and feel for finesse than others. But you can improve your touch with two fun practice routines.

1) Play mini-tennis. Hitting each shot on the first bounce, rally with your practice partner inside the service lines. As you improve, make the ball bounce twice—in essence, a rally of nothing but drop shots. You'll quickly learn what you need to do to hit the ball softer. You'll also gain a much greater feel for controlling your racquet head.

2) Catch the ball on the strings. This is the ultimate example of taking pace off the ball. As you are positioned at the net, have your practice partner feed you the ball from his forecourt. Instead of bunting the volley back to him, soften your grip and twist the racquet head open at contact so you catch the ball with it, like a lacrosse player. This drill is excellent practice for drop volleys.

COMPETING

THE PLAYING FIELD

1. The Safer Shot

When in doubt, hit the ball crosscourt. It is the safer shot for three reasons. One, the net is six inches lower in the center than at the sidelines. Two, when you hit cross-court from baseline corner to baseline corner, the ball can fly 82½ feet before going long. When you hit down the line from corner to corner, the ball can fly only 78 feet before going long. Three, when you aim crosscourt the ball can veer off-line and stay in because of the large angle you are hitting into, whereas if you aim straight down the line and the ball veers off a little to the side, it will go wide.

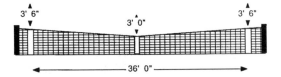

Net Height: The net is six inches lower at the center than at the sidelines.

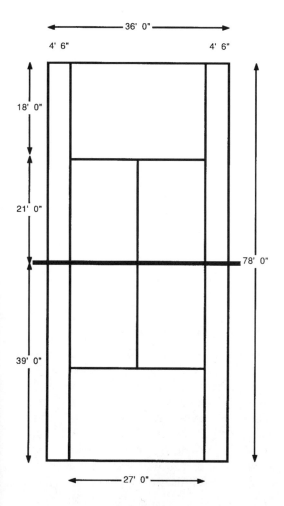

Court Dimensions: The safer crosscourt shot can travel 4½ feet farther than a down-the-line-shot and stay in.

EIGHT SIMPLE STRATEGY IDEAS

1. Get Back One More Ball

Except in the elite ranks, errors, not winners, decide tennis matches. So on every point make it a priority to give your opponent one more chance to miss.

2. Hammer Your Opponent's Weakness

First, your relentless attack will prey on his mind, forcing him into tentative, indecisive shot-making. Second, you increase the chances his shot will collapse completely. And third, you reduce your own decision making on every point. For most club players, the backhand is the weaker side; that's where you should direct your attack.

3. Play Safe with Your Weakness

When the tables are turned, your job is to stay out of trouble with your weakness. So go into the match with a game plan. If, for instance, your backhand is your weakness, decide that every time you hit one you are going to go crosscourt and deep. Then all you'll have to do is concentrate on making a good swing. You will be predictable, but that's a better alternative to being error-prone.

4. Hit Deep and Down the Middle

It's the strategy used by pushers all over the world, and they're the ones with all the trophies. Deep and down the middle does three things. First, it eliminates three of the four places you might miss: the net (because the easiest way to get depth is to hit the ball higher over the net) and the two sidelines. Second, it backs your opponent up behind the baseline so he can't attack you. Third, it reduces the angles your opponent has to work with on his reply.

5. Four "1-2" Tactical Combinations

These patterns are riskier but still simple. *Right-left:* Run your opponent ragged from corner to corner. Then, once he starts to overanticipate, hit behind him by going back to the same corner twice in a row. *Long-short:* Drive your opponent back with a deep ball, then when he returns short, hit a drop shot. If he reaches it, lob over his head. *High-low:* Loop a topspin so your opponent has to reach up, then hit a sharp slice that forces him to bend way down. Move the ball up and down in his strike zone like a baseball pitcher. *Hard-soft:* Drive one shot then float the next one. Prevent your opponent from getting into a smooth stroking rhythm.

6. Rally Crosscourt, Approach Down the Line

When you are exchanging shots from the baseline, it's technically harder to change the direction of the ball and return a crosscourt shot straight down the line than to change the direction of the ball and return a down-the-line shot crosscourt. Rallying crosscourt reduces your chances of making an error (see **The Safer Shot**, p.118). Also, you don't open up your side of the court to angled returns from your opponent if you return crosscourt the way you do when hitting down the line.

When your opponent hits short, however, it's wiser to play your approach shot down the line. Your straight shot gives him less time to chase it down. If you've been in a crosscourt rallying pattern, he has farther to run for your approach. And when you run in and set up at the net, you are right in the middle of his angles of possible returns (on a crosscourt approach you'd have to run in farther—diagonally to the other side of the center service line—to cut off his much wider passing-shot angles). There are two times to break the down-the-line approach rule: 1) When the opponent's crosscourt side is glaringly weaker and 2) when you have a big lead in a game and you want to break your approach pattern to keep from being predictable.

7. Take One Chance per Point

In almost every exchange, you will have a chance to go for a big shot. The key is recognizing when. Usually the right time is when your opponent has hit short and high, so you can move forward and hit down (meaning you can contact the ball comfortably above the level of the net) and away from him. That's when you should go for it. And once you've got him in trouble, move in even farther for the kill.

8. Bail Out of Trouble

When you're the one scrambling, the temptation is to go for an all-or-nothing winner from a bad position. Resist the temptation and throw up a high defensive lob instead. It gives your opponent another chance to miss and it gives you time to recover your court position and stay in the point if he doesn't miss.

EIGHT MENTAL REMINDERS

1. Play One Point at a Time

Tennis is hard enough as it is without wasting energy worrying about what you cannot control. You can't change the result of the previous point and you can't win the next point until it begins. Moreover, if you look back you may get discouraged, and if you look ahead you may get scared. So focus all your concentration on the point you are playing now.

2. Play the Ball, Not Your Opponent

Your opponent may have a reputation for being unbeatable, for being unflappable, for being annoying. But it is his shots that you have to contend with, not his record or personality. As soon as you begin thinking about him instead of your game, he has you at a disadvantage. So keep your eyes and effort focused on the ball, not the individual hitting it.

3. Follow a Between-Point Routine

A natural response to pressure is rushing. Following the same ritual point after point helps you slow down. You immediately have an emotional reaction at the end of almost every point. You then have to recover from the stress of that point and relax from the demands of concentrating during play for an entire match. Put your racquet in your other hand and take a stroll toward your next ready position, perhaps straightening the strings or doing something else that keeps your eyes from getting distracted by outside events. As you get close to the ready position, make sure you know the score and plan the next point. Finally, get set to play. If you are serving, bounce the ball a few times and pause before you start to swing. If you are receiving, shuffle your feet and pause as you focus your eyes on your opponent's tossing hand. The server must play at a reasonable pace, and the receiver must keep up with that pace. Repeating the same routine every time will give you a feel of control even when the pressure is intense.

4. Take a Deep Breath

Before serving or getting set to receive, take a deep breath and exhale. It will settle your nerves and help your muscles relax.

5. Stick to a Plan

You should have an overall strategy when you start the match, such as serving and volleying, drawing your opponent to the net when receiving, and playing to your opponent's backhand during rallies. You also should have a more specific plan before each point, such as slicing the serve wide and hitting the first volley crosscourt. When you step up to the line to play, stick to the plan. It will reduce your decision making during the point, letting you focus only on the proper execution of the shot.

Your goal is to dictate the pattern of play, not be forced to improvise in reaction to your opponent's shots.

6. Move Your Feet

When you get nervous you tend to go flatfooted, so when things get tight, make sure you keep your weight forward on the balls of your feet and always keep your feet moving toward the ball, taking that extra step to get into position for perfect execution.

7. Play Your Hardest

If you give a 100 percent effort and still lose, you can walk away from the match feeling good about yourself. You may need to go back and work on your game, but you won't need to make any excuses for yourself. You'll know that your opponent has won the match, that you didn't beat yourself.

8. Have Fun

Tennis is a game. It's play. If you don't have fun, why go out there in the first place?

PLAYING LEFTIES

1. Be Prepared

It's surprising how often a player doesn't realize his opponent is left-handed until the match is well underway. Pay attention during the warm-up. All of a lefty's spins will curve the opposite way from a right-hander's. And his backhand will be on his right side, meaning the pattern of cross-court rallies are your forehand to his backhand and vice versa.

2. Step Left to Receive

The left-hander serve right-handers fear most, and with reason, is the sweeping wide slice to their backhands, especially in the ad court. To counteract it, set up to receive at least a full step to the left of where you usually take your ready position, with one foot in the doubles alley on the ad side. Concede the serve down the center to your forehand until you are being beaten by it regularly.

3. Squeeze Tight

The unfamiliar left-handed spin will make the ball shoot off your strings in all directions if you don't make a firm stroke. So hold the handle tight at impact to keep your shot on line.

C
O
M
P
E
T
I
N
G

4. Do Unto the Lefty . . .

Turnabout is fair play. Just as the left-hander's slice serve breaks wide to your backhand in the ad court, so too does your slice serve break wide to his backhand in the deuce court. So run him out of court with your serve. If you serve and volley, shade to your left as you close in, looking for a down-the-line return that you can volley with a backhand crosscourt into the hole you've opened.

5. Read the Lefty's Forehand Grip

Classic left-handers often use a Continental grip, with the hand on top of the racquet handle. When you see that, be ready for a lot of sharp crosscourt forehands to your backhand. Shade left as the Continental lefty begins his backswing. More modern lefties often use a semi-Western grip, with the hand way under the racquet handle. When you see that, look for more heavy topspin forehands and more inside-out forehands hit toward your forehand corner. The semi-Western lefty especially likes to run around the backhand and hit the inside-out shot. Hold your position in the middle of the court during a rally.

6. Lob into the Sun

When the sun is glaring down on your right side on serves and overheads, it's in a similarly tough place above the lefty's left side on his side of the net. So use the advantage and lob him when he's over there. He may miss the overhead or at least be forced to let the lob bounce.

COURT SURFACES

1. Hard Courts

Expect a consistent bounce of medium height at a medium to fast pace. Beware that the smoother the court, the lower and quicker the bounce, whereas the rougher the court, the higher and slower the bounce. The surface can be sort of sticky, so pick up your feet as you move. Mix up your serves, using flat, slice, and topspin. Shorten your backswing a little on ground strokes, and more than a little if the court is really fast. Serve and volley regularly if it's your style. Attack any short ball, using slice approach shots. Force the action without becoming reckless.

2. Clay Courts

Expect a high, slow bounce and slippery footing. Be prepared for a few bad bounces, such as when the ball hits the tape lines. Use a topspin serve and topspin ground strokes. Aim higher for more depth. Take the racquet back higher to be ready for the high bounces. Hit behind your opponent. Attack only at optimum opportunities and stay alert for your put-aways to come back because your opponent has more time to get to the ball. Use the drop shot. Learn to slide by "skating" into the shot, stopping just as you hit. Above all, be patient and work the point.

3. Grass Courts

Expect a low, fast, inconsistent bounce and slippery footing. Be ready to react to more *really* bad bounces than usual. Use a slice serve and play serve-and-volley. Chip your returns and consider following the low ones to the net. Whenever possible move forward and hit the ball in the air. Bend your knees. Use a really short, early backswing on ground strokes. Hit all forcing shots away from your opponent so the ball skids away. Use the drop volley, which won't bounce much. Play with a quick-strike attitude.

4. Indoor Courts

Whether the court is hard and fast or soft (clay) and slow, take advantage of your surroundings. Even clay will play faster indoors than outdoors because it will probably have less topping and be drier. Check

Whether the court is hard and fast or soft (clay) and slow, take advantage of your surroundings. Even clay will play faster indoors than outdoors because it will probably have less topping and be drier. Check out the ceiling height and light locations, then be judicious in hitting defensive lobs. (You lose the point if the ball hits any part of the building.) Change positions at the baseline if you have trouble with glare from the lights and watch the ball especially closely on returns, volleys, and overheads. Run your opponent into the side netting with slice serves and angled volleys. Make him feel hemmed in. It's fair. Remember he can do the same to you, so play the ball on the rise.

A DOZEN DOUBLES IDEAS

1. Selecting Receiving Sides

There are no definitive rules, but there are several theories, including: One, the toughest return in doubles is the inside-out crosscourt backhand from the deuce court, so the player with the better backhand should play there. Two, the middle is the most vulnerable spot on the court, so the player with the better forehand and overhead should play the ad court. It is also easier for him to run around his backhand return and hit a forehand on that side. Three, the steadier ball-control returner from ad-in lead with one swing of the racquet. Superseding all those is personal preference. If one player simply feels more comfortable on one side and the other player doesn't have a strong preference, put the first player where he likes to be.

2. Get the First Serve In

A big first serve will come back at you as fast as you hit it, giving you less time to get to the net. And you'll miss it a lot, giving your opponents too many looks at second serves. A safer spin serve gives you more time to get to the net and its higher success rate keeps the mental pressure on your opponents. Vary the placement of your serve consistently.

3. Return Low and Crosscourt

If you hit straight at the net man, he'll put the ball away. If you hit hard and high to the incoming server, he has an easy first volley. Put the ball on his shoelaces so he has to hit up to you.

4. Command the Net

Whether you are the server or the returner, move forward to join your partner at net as fast as you can. The closer you are to the net, the more you can hit down on your opponents and the more angle you have to hit into. Try to move forward after every shot, with the idea in mind that you'll end the point by hitting a winning volley from right on top of the net. The team that controls the net won't win every point, but it will have the better chance of winning every point.

5. Poach

Be an active net man. If your partner is serving, you should stay put sometimes and sometimes move out, just as the receiver begins his forward swing, to cut off the return. At other times bluff like you're going to poach and then stay. You may be rewarded with an easy sitter. The best times to poach are when your partner hits a strong serve to the receiver's weaker side or when your partner jams the receiver with the serve. If you are the receiver's partner, move out to poach when your partner hits a sharp, low return that forces the net-rushing server to either half-volley or volley up. Whenever the poacher crosses the center service line, he should keep going and his partner should cross over behind him to cover the vacated side of the court. Poaching may cost you a few points, but you'll win more, you'll keep your opponents off balance, and you'll have fun.

6. Keep Them Honest

The doubles alleys are each 4½ feet wide. Don't ignore that extra 9 feet of court. Crosscourt and down-the-middle shots are the safest in doubles, but to avoid being totally predictable, hit down the line from time to time. It's one way to foil a poacher. Hit at least one return down-the-line in each of your opponents' first service games to let the net men know you intend to keep them honest.

7. Hit Down the Middle

When in doubt in doubles, go down the middle. First, it's got the most margin for error—you can only miss in the net or long, not right or left. Second, it reduces your opponents' angle of return. Third, it opens up more angles to you on the sides. And fourth, it can create confusion between your opponents about who should return your shot.

8. Handling Low and High Volleys

Whenever you are volleying from below the level of the net tape, play the ball back to the opponent who is farther back. It's also the safer play on medium-height volleys. On high volleys, though, hit down aggressively at the closer player's feet.

9. Lob

Drive your opponents back from the net by going over their heads. As soon as they turn to chase your lob, you and your partner should move into the forecourt. A lob service return over the net man should be a regular part of your arsenal. It's also the other way to foil a poacher.

10. Move Together

You and your partner should move in tandem, like windshield wipers. If the ball is wide left, move left together so the inside player covers the middle as the outside player hits the shot. If the ball is wide right, move right together. If a lob goes over your heads, move back together. Imagine there is a rope connecting you. Keep the rope taut at all times except when you move toward each other to cover a ball down the middle.

11. Different Formations

Except at the start of the point, when-ever possible you and your partner should be virtually equidistant from the net. The best formation is for both partners to be at the net. The next best is for both to be at the baseline, which reduces your oppo-nents' targets because you are in a defen-sive alignment. The worst formation is one player up and one player back, which is also the most common among club players. It gives your net-rushing opponents the option of hitting in the big hole between the two of you, hitting down at the sitting duck net man, or hitting an angled volley way in front of the backcourt player. An option for thc serving team at the start of the point is the Australian or tandem formation. The net man assumes his fore-court position on the same side as the server, who moves in diagonally to cover the open court after his delivery. Use this alignment to counter a receiver who is beating you regularly with his crosscourt returns.

12. Communicate

Talk positively to each other between points to pump each other up and to plan strategy. Avoid apologizing or criticizing. Use hand signals behind your back to let your serving partner know if you are going to poach. Help your partner by calling "Mine," "Yours," or "Out" on close balls during the point (such quick commands are allowed, provided the ball is moving in your direction when you speak). Finally, remember you win as a team *and* you lose as a team.

EIGHT STICKY RULES SITUATIONS

1. Spinning for Serve

Many players believe they have three choices if they win the spin: serving, receiving, or selecting sides (if you pick sides, your opponent may either serve or receive). There's a fourth option: having your opponent make the first choice.

2. Close Calls

In an unofficiated match, United States Tennis Association regulations say that if you are unsure whether your opponent's shot was in or out, you must give him the benefit of the doubt and call it good. When you correct a mistaken "out" call to "in" after seeing a mark on a clay court, you lose the point whether your return was in the net or out, and you replay the point if your return was good. When you believe your opponent is blatantly cheating, ask for an umpire if it is a tournament match. Use personal discretion about questioning bad calls in an unofficial match (you might request your opponent show you a mark if you're playing on clay). Under no circumstances should you make a retaliatory bad call. If the situation ruins your enjoyment of the match, don't play that opponent again.

3. Foot Faults

It's the most abused rule in tennis. You have the right to call your opponent for a foot fault after warning him if you are certain he's stepping on or over the baseline before striking the ball. That's hard to do in singles, however, where you should focus on the ball being served, not the opponent's feet. In doubles, the receiver's partner can call foot faults with more surety. Even though foot-faulting is cheating, it is rarely monitored in non-tournament play.

4. Calling a Let

The rule is often misapplied. Aside from when a serve hits the net and lands in the proper court (entitling the player to another first serve or another second serve), call a let when there's outside interference during the point (a ball rolling into your court from elsewhere in the middle of a rally, players walking behind your court during the point, and so on), when a ball breaks in play, or when your opponent inadvertently hinders you from making your shot (if he does something intentionally, like yelling to distract you, he loses the point). When the receiver causes a delay between first and second serves, the server gets to take two. When the server causes such a delay, he gets only his second serve. When there is outside interference between serves, such as a ball rolling into the court, it's the receiver's prerogative whether to grant a let. Unless the interruption is quite brief, the fair thing to do is give the server two serves. You cannot call a let by claiming you weren't ready for your opponent's serve if you make any attempt to return the serve. And finally, you absolutely cannot call a let either after a point has ended or when you are unsure of a call. If you are unsure, you must give the benefit of the doubt to your opponent and call the ball good.

5. You Lose the Point If . . .

A point is lost if you, your racquet, your clothes, or any other part of your equipment (such as a string-vibration damper that pops out) touches the net or your opponent's court during the point; you hit the ball before it crosses the net to your side; the ball hits you before it bounces, whether you are standing inside or outside the court (you cannot catch an out ball on the fly behind the baseline); the ball hits a stray ball lying inside the lines on your side and you cannot make the return; or if you throw your racquet at the ball to make a safe return.

6. But You Can . . .

You can follow through across the net if you don't touch it; reach across the net to hit a ball that's bounced on your side and spun back over (you lose the point if you fail to hit the ball before it lands again on your opponent's side or if you touch the net while hitting it); serve underhand; crowd the service line when receiving; change receiving positions during your opponent's toss, provided you don't wave, stomp your feet, yell, or otherwise intentionally hinder him; and hit the ball around the net post, even below the level of the net tape, when pulled wide.

7. Double Hit

This shot is legal when you make one continuous swing, even if the ball seems to be "carried" on the strings. It is illegal when you make a definite or deliberate second push at the ball.

8. Losing Track of the Score

When there is a discrepancy as to what the score is, go back to the point where you and your opponent agree and try to reconstruct the points together from there. If you cannot agree past a certain point, replay the disputed points from there. To avoid it in the first place, the USTA rulebook says that the server should call the set score clearly before beginning the game and call the point score clearly before beginning each subsequent point in the game.

HOW TO PLAY A TIEBREAKER

1. The Rules

Play a tiebreaker when the set score reaches 6–6. Player A, who served first in the set, serves the first tiebreaker point into the deuce court. Player B serves the next two points, the first to the ad court. Player A serves the fourth and fifth points, the first to the ad court. Player B serves the sixth point to the ad court, then the players change ends. Player B serves the seventh point to the deuce court. Player A serves the eighth and ninth points, the first to the ad court. Player B serves the tenth and eleventh points, the first to the ad court. Player A serves the twelfth point to the ad court. The first player to win seven points by a margin of two wins the tiebreaker. If the score is tied at 6–6, the players change ends again with Player A serving the thirteenth point to the deuce court, and the pattern continues.

Three things to remember: First, after the first point, each two-point serving rotation begins with a delivery to the ad court. Second, the players must change ends after every six points. Third, the player who served the second game of the set serves the first game of the following set.

2. The Strategy

Every point counts, so maintain peak concentration. Get your first serve in. There's so much pressure that you are more likely to double-fault if you force yourself to hit a lot of second serves. Your opponent faces similar pressure on his serve points, so get your returns in play. Don't give him any free points. Play aggressively but not recklessly. Work the points to force an error rather than simply play passive, just-get-it-back tennis. Play at a deliberate pace, taking time to regroup between points instead of rushing. Finally, approach the tiebreaker with confidence and project that with upbeat body language and no negative displays of emotion.

PRACTICE

1. Drills

Recreational players don't practice enough, and when they do, they don't practice efficiently. The way to improve is through structured practice, not random hitting. Assume your regular, weekly, singles game goes for an hour and a half. Once a month, turn it into a practice session instead. Divide the first hour of practice time into five-minute segments. Use the first five minutes to loosen up with easy rallying. Then do a series of five-minute drills. For ground strokes, rally crosscourt forehand to crosscourt forehand, crosscourt backhand to crosscourt backhand, down-the-line forehand to down-the-line backhand, and down-the-line backhand to down-the-line forehand (20 minutes). For volleys, rally crosscourt forehand volley to crosscourt forehand, then crosscourt backhand volley to crosscourt backhand, followed by the same two patterns with the other player at net (20 minutes). Then hit five minutes of overheads each, followed by five minutes of hitting practice serves back and forth. Then use the last half hour of your practice session to play a match. Rather than play a conventional set, though, use alternative scoring systems so you get a concentrated dose of competition that allows you to work on specific shots and puts a premium on concentrating on each point.

2. 21

Play games to twenty-one points, changing serves after every five points like Ping Pong and changing ends after every ten points. Employ handicaps if one player is better than the other, like a golfer giving strokes. Also, adjust the scoring to reward success on specific plays you are working on. One example would be to practice hitting winners, in which a clean winner would earn two points compared to just one for an error. Another would be to practice going to the net, in which a point won by the player who finishes the rally in the forecourt would earn two points.

3. Tiebreakers

Play the best-of-three or the best-of-five tiebreakers, depending on how much time you have. It will force you to focus on each practice point and will help you get more comfortable with the format and pressure of tiebreakers when you play them in actual matches.

CONDITIONING

1. Fitness

For stamina, do three 30-minute aerobic workouts a week (jogging, cycling, fast walking). For quickness, jump rope for 15 minutes three times a week or run the lines of the court at full sprint speed regularly. For strength, do three 30-minute calesthenic workouts a week, doing sit-ups for the stomach muscles and push-ups for the arms and upper body. If you do weight work, either on machines or with free weights, three supervised sessions a week is plenty, but not on the days you play. Lift light weights and do more repetitions.

Tennis players need muscular speed, flexibility, and endurance as well as gross strength, so avoid bulking up. The only place where heavier lifts can help tennis players is in the legs, because leg strength translates into better quickness. Finally, for flexibility, stretch at least 15 minutes daily. Jog in place or jump rope for a few minutes before you start stretching. And *always* stretch before and after a match.

2. Nutrition

A healthy way to improve court coverage and stamina for the majority of recreational players would be to take off five to ten pounds through more sensible eating habits. The best tennis diets are high in complex carbohydrates (fruits, vegetables, breads, grains) and low in fats. A pasta dinner the night before a big match, and a breakfast of grain cereal and fresh fruit the morning of the match are ideal. Equally important to eating right is drinking enough fluids. Dehydration through perspiration can easily afflict tennis players, leading to cramps and more severe illnesses due to overheating. Drink plenty of water. At a minimum, begin with a couple of large glasses an hour before a match, continue with sips on every changeover during play, and drink large amounts, beyond the point of satisfying your thirst, after you finish. If you have an important match the next day and high temperature is predicted, start drinking water the night before, downing a glass an hour up until match time. Avoid alcohol, caffeine, and salt pills.

EQUIPMENT

1. Overview

The essentials of tennis equipment—racquets, strings, and shoes—have undergone profound changes during the last decade and a half. Every year manufacturers come out with new models for which they make eye-opening claims of enhanced playability—a few true, many not true. The only element of the equipment equation that remains above the hype and continues to fulfill its role to everyone's satisfaction is the ball. Here are a few hints at getting the most from the rest of your gear.

2. Racquets

Head sizes. They can be divided into two basic categories: midsize—racquets with up to 100 square inches of hitting area; and oversize, racquets with more than 100 square inches of hitting area. Within those two groups, some are marketed as midplus (90 –100 square inches) and superoversize (above 110 square inches). While matching a racquet to a player's game is a highly subjective exercise, some general guidelines can be prescribed. Midsize racquets are better suited for more skilled players who hit the center of the strings more often; for physically powerful players who generate pace with their long, smooth strokes; for players who want a racquet that is quite manueverable, especially on serves and volleys; and for players who want an exceptionally even, consistent response from the string bed. Oversize racquets are better suited for less-skilled players who need a big hitting surface to make good contact; for less powerful players who want the racquet to enhance the pace of their short, punchy strokes; for players who want a racquet they can just put in front of the ball to block it, with a reasonable expectation that it will go back over the net without twisting off-line; and for players who want a string bed that will "trampoline" the ball back.

Wide-bodies. The most important and most visible change in racquets since the advent of the oversize racquet has been the introduction of wide-body frames, which are decidely thicker than traditional racquets when viewed from the side. Wide-bodies are stiffer and thus more powerful than traditional racquets. But they are not all created equal. Manufacturers sculpt the shape of the frame in different ways to provide different flex patterns. In general, the fatter the frame, the more powerful it will be. But the power potential can vary depending on the ratio of materials used. A 100 percent graphite frame will be stiffer and thus more powerful than a frame of identical shape made of a composite blend of graphite and fiberglass. A sensible way to decide on a new racquet is to talk to an experienced pro-shop operator and test a handful of different demonstration models he recommends based on your description of your playing style.

Lead tape. You can customize the play-ability of your racquet by adding strips of lead tape (sold in most pro shops) to the racquet head. Putting tape at the tip of the head will raise the sweet spot and give the frame a more head-heavy balance and more powerful playability. You can broaden the sweet spot and help stabilize the racquet on off-center hits by adding the tape at the 3 o'clock and 9 o'clock positions on the head. Add tape at the 2 o'clock and 10 o'clock positions to achieve both objectives. If you want to get the benefits of lead tape while keeping the racquet's balance the same, add similar amounts of tape to the handle area. And if you want to give your racquet a more head-light balance, add tape only at the handle.

3. Strings

String patterns. A denser string grid, one with more strings and, consequently, smaller openings between them, will produce a firmer, more controlled, more predictable playing response. A more open pattern, with fewer strings and larger openings, will have a livelier playability and give you greater potential for spin because it grips the ball better. But the strings saw against each other more in an open pattern, so they tend to break more quickly. When buying a racquet, consider how the density of the string pattern matches up with your style of play.

String types. Most synthetic strings are made of nylon, despite the marketing moniker of "synthetic gut" applied to some. They offer a whole range of playability and durability, although none can match natural gut in the former characteristic while virtually all exceed natural gut in the latter. A qualified stringer can explain the differences to you. Natural gut has a resiliency, texture, and playability unmatched by any synthetic strings. But you will pay around $20 more for gut than for synthetic, and the string job won't last as long. Whichever type of string you choose, another factor to consider is the

C
O
M
P
E
T
I
N
G

string's gauge, or thickness. A thick string (15 or 16 gauge) will be durable and deliver a firm response. A thinner string (16L or 17 gauge) will wear out faster but will deliver a livelier response and greater spin potential.

Tension. If you don't know how tight you want your strings, begin in the center of the racquet manufacturer's recommended range. The rule of thumb to follow is string tighter for more control, looser for more power. Looser strings also will help cushion the shock of the racquet's impact with the ball before it reaches your arm, but they also will move more, so they may break sooner.

Restringing. Even if your strings don't break, they will lose their tension and resiliency over time. One formula to follow is to restring as many times in a year as you play in a week.When you take your racquet in to be restrung, have the stringer check the grommets for wear and tear. A split grommet can cause an annoying rattle or even cut the string.

Vibration dampers. Those little foam balls or rubber donuts you insert between the strings reduce the vibration of the strings and muffle the "ping" sound of impact, which is particularly sharp in stiffer racquets. A vibration damper will *not* reduce the shock and vibration of the racquet frame itself or prevent that shock from reaching your arm. The rules specify that a damper must be placed outside the pattern of crossed strings. The best place to put it is between the two center main, or vertical, strings below the bottom cross string.

4. Grips

Synthetics and overwraps. The traditional leather grip is rapidly going the way of the traditional-width racquet. Taking its place are synthetic grips that first emerged as replacement grips but are now factory installed on many racquets. They offer superior stickiness (the pores of leather grips get clogged with sweat, making the surface slippery over time, while most synthetics can easily be wiped clean) and cushioning. Many synthetic grips are backed with padding so your hand sinks in a little as you squeeze. This feature helps reduce the shock of impact. Synthetics come with a variety of surface textures, such as perforations or ribbing. Most types of synthetic replacement are easy to install yourself. The other option in grips is to use an overwrap. It goes on over the factory installed grip. If you use a thicker overwrap, you may want to buy a racquet one handle-size smaller than you like. Regrip at least as often as you restring for optimum playability.

5. Shoes

When to buy new ones. A hole in the sole or the toe is the obvious indicator. But you should also monitor the structural integrity of the rest of the shoe. When the upper becomes really stretched out or sags perceptibly, it is no longer supporting your foot properly. And when the midsole, the layer between the outer sole and upper, becomes compressed (evident by a narrowing of its thickness) it is no longer cushioning your foot properly. In either case, it's time to buy new shoes.

3/4-cut models. Tennis's answer to the basketball high-top is an excellent choice for players whose feet roll inward excessively (overpronation) or don't roll enough; who need extra ankle support or a better fit; or who use custom-made orthotics.

Orthotics. Active players with high arches or other foot chacteristics that need extra support, or who experience discomfort in the feet, ankles, knees, legs, hips, or lower back, should experiment with over-the-counter insoles in place of the factory-supplied sockliner or insole. If the problem persists, they should consider doctor-prescribed, custom-made insoles, known as orthotics.

THE AUTHORS

Alexander McNab was editor of *Tennis* magazine from 1986 to 1990. He joined the staff in 1979 after three years as managing editor of *Tennis USA,* and still serves as a contributing editor. He has also written about the sport for the *New York Times* and *Sports Illustrated.* He is accredited as an instructor by the U.S. Professional Tennis Registry teaching pro organization.

Michael Brent, an independent illustrator and designer, was art director and then graphics director of *Tennis* magazine from 1978 to 1987.

INDEX